TAKE ME HOME, WINDRIDER

JEFF KNIGHTON

TAKE ME HOME, WINDRIDER

-   "One Cowboy's Perspective"

JEFF KNIGHTON

Baal Hamon Publishers
Akure, Nigeria.

For permissions and any other enquiries, please write to Baal Hamon Publishers, P. O. Box 2338, Akure, Ondo State, Nigeria.

www.baalhamon.com/publishers/

publishers@baalhamon.com

ISBN : 978-978-49565-0-5

TAKE ME HOME, WINDRIDER

"One Cowboy's Perspective"

When I was a child I thought as a child and wanted to be another Lenny Moore, #24 with the Baltimore Colts! Then I decided I wanted to be my band-director dad and play my beloved tuba for the rest of my life.

Then I grew up a bit more and wanted to be a cowboy, or an Indian – it didn't matter which. I just wanted to live in the great outdoors and go everywhere on the back of a mighty and trustworthy horse.

As time has flown by, I've lived in and through years of labor in such diverse ways as farming and ranching, teaching, print and radio media work, carpentry, and finally ministry – the place I've worked longest and been blessed most abundantly.

And while ministry fulfills my calling and purpose in life, never have I forgotten those early dreams and experiences. In fact, each has informed my growth and maturation in ministry. In addition, I am thankful for skills I still use, and for invitations I've received to participate in using some of those cowboy and writing skills through these years as a Pastor.

For these gifts I am deeply appreciative, especially as they find themselves woven into my preaching and teaching, and for how those cowboy dreams and ranching experiences have made TAKE ME HOME, WINDRIDER both possible and a reality.

CONTENTS

"A Traveler's Tale"

Jeremiah 1:5; Exodus 9:16

"I knew you before your mama knew you were on the way!"

The new day was a welcome relief. A cool morning breeze was clean and invigorating, totally opposite the unusual heat of yesterday. As I headed for the barn to saddle Deuce I was looking forward to riding pasture in these early conditions, even knowing that they could well give way to another afternoon of dusty depression.

I was off to the northwest pasture to check mama cows and their new babies while Tom, foreman on the LZ ranch, was headed to the southeast; both of us were looking for any signs of sickness, or even maybe the birth of a new calf. It was about a three-mile ride out, the needed time riding the pasture, and then the ride back.

Sights and sounds and smells along the way captured my imagination. The breeze through the tops of creek-bottom cottonwoods and the trickle of clear water over multi-colored stones, the songs of birds and crickets, the greening of late

Spring, and the smell of leather over horse flesh were together a lush symphony to the senses, a blessing of Mother Nature's own design.

My work was completed with only one stop to doctor the beginnings of pinkeye in a very young calf, so the journey back to the house would get me there just in time for another of Mary Francis' amazing lunches.

Tom's mom, we call her MF, was a tiny lady who wielded wide influence among the family and crew, in part because of her poetic view of creation and faith, work and leisure. She was a delight with whom I shared many an evening hour in conversation regarding ultimate matters such as life, death, purpose, and passion. And she was an incredible cook to boot.

About a mile from the barn I was daydreaming, thankful for the rodeo-free morning and the comfortable weather. As I rode up over a rise that would bring the home place into view I happened to glance down at the ground. I don't know why, but when I looked there I was startled to see a beautiful wild flower, Indian blanket we call it, decked out in bright orange, red and yellow in its daisy formation. I had seen thousands, no millions of these small beauties on this ranch, but this one struck me in a unique way.

I pulled Deuce to a stop and stepped down. Kneeling beside that new-found treasure, I realized for the first time that many wild flowers such as this one had been born, blossomed, and died without ever being seen by human eyes. What made this one so special was that I noticed it, causing me to wonder if it was there just for me!

Of course it was there with or without my surprise, but in that moment it was mine, and I was thankful. It was a gift that reminded me of God's glorious grace everywhere. Instead of plucking it for a hatband ornament, I left it in honor of that grace.

That was a transformational moment for me, an experience that I believe nurtures my faith travels even today. For that gift became a vital ingredient in my journey's blossoming into a question that now captivates my imagination.

I have come to wonder: are we indeed known by God before we are created in our mother's womb, and stamped by God with a divine purpose for this journey? Are we truly created only a little less than the angels; and as we travel this life as sojourners in a foreign land, could it be possible that we are invited to participate in a gift the angels don't receive? Could it be possible that our returning to the home we call Heaven is angel-anticipated, and that upon our arrival we will be welcomed to a forum where we might describe to the angels what this human experience has been like for us?

Could it be that in our human separation from home we come to know something about grace and glory that angels can't know?

Is it possible that we're invited to participate in this journey into a strange and faraway place so that in our return home we can share with the angels what it's like to find and glorify God in the surprise of simple wildflowers along the way that assure us God is yet present and worthy of our praise, no matter where we are? Could it possibly be true?

The more I experiment with the thought and apply it to my daily life, the more it makes sense to me. And how exciting it is to consider divine ramifications and shared angel-joy as my unique story – or indeed each of our stories – is told.

Even beyond that, it thrills me to believe that my

response of praise, of offering the glory due to God, could be created in any form I choose! I dream now about the possibility of being given a Heaven-gift of musical skill beyond my present limitations so I might compose a symphony of praise scored for a full band and orchestra and chorus of heavenly musicians, maybe angel talents!

With Handel having already produced his "Messiah," I wouldn't need to rework that masterpiece. I could produce a gift specific to my journey's discoveries, one that will speak to the glory of God in the many and different ways I have found God present to me in good times and not so good, in health or sickness, in pain or pleasure all along the way home.

To top that off, if I choose to do so, I might simultaneously conduct the complete work myself while astride a perfectly gentle horse and playing along on the tuba!

Surely this sojourn is an adventure planned in Heaven, and for those who accept the blessings, an opportunity to thrill even the angels upon our return with reports of God's glory discovered everywhere, even in lone wildflowers far, far from home.

"A Traveler's Tale"

JEREMIAH 1:5

It looks simple enough: Jeremiah has received a call and commission from God, and the Lord's assurance to him is that *"You have come from me, you began as an idea in my heart, 'before you saw the light of day, I had holy plans for you' (Mssg), you are to be a prophet to all my children who also came from the same place as yourself!"*

In other words, Jeremiah has, and we all have, come into being out of the creative genius and unlimited love of God.

And while we are not all prophets, I believe it's safe to believe we all are called and commissioned by God for a specific purpose.

EXODUS 9:16

In the midst of his instruction to Moses, the Lord notes that Moses has been allowed to live for one purpose: that God's almighty power might be seen, and God's very name sounded throughout all creation, "*that my reputation spreads in all the earth*" (Mssg).

In other words, Moses was, and we are, called to offer evidence of God's glory in the lives we live: in our thoughts, words, and deeds. And in order that we do that, we must look for it, search our minds, hearts, and spirits in the midst of this earthly experience to find and reveal evidences of God's unlimited power, love, grace, and mercy!

REFLECTIONS

So, if we've come from somewhere (Heaven), and we are given a divine mission or plan to fulfill, it seems appropriate to believe that when we get back home a part of our mission might be to compile a glory/grace/power/love report to share with the angels, those divine among our brothers and sisters who are not given the gift of the human journey into this wilderness, to report to them and all of Heaven how amazing is God's power and grace even when separated from home!

Do you believe you came from the creative hand of God?

Do you believe God has a plan, a commission for you to fulfill here on earth?

How often do you find God's amazing grace there to

bless you, whether you are celebrating the joys of life or groaning under the weight of life's challenges?

How often do you report to your circle of influence these evidences of God's intimate presence to you, in both the good times and the challenging times?

If you were to begin writing down evidence of God's presence and grace in your life, how long do you think it might take you to have a gigantic journal of celebrated comfort and peace and joy collected?

"Riding on the Sky"

Acts 1:6-11
"They stood speechless, gawking at the empty sky."

The privilege of riding a pasture with wildflowers apparently strategically placed just for my edification and amazement was afforded me by long time family friends, the Ellzey family.

On their ranch I grew up with their youngest son Stephen. Now I realize I was having a blast shocking feed for 5-cents an hour, gathering eggs, watching him milk the cow, and cleaning out the stock trailers because I was invited to be there, while he endured what he had to do!

I was given a wondrous gift in his patience through my weekly childhood post-church questioning, *"Are you going to the ranch today?"*, asked with the hope of an invitation to join him!

I just don't remember a day in my life that I haven't been deeply in love with that place, with that family, and with the gift it was and is to know those days with fondly vivid recall.

It was there that I fell in love with horses and the cowboy life. And it was there I became fascinated by the stories I heard, and the pictures I saw of Stephen's dad, Lawrence, and his brothers. I loved all four of them for different reasons, and was simply fascinated by what I learned about Jack, the one I'm told was the best horse trainer among them. Jack was the one who trained his paint to shake, to roll over, to sit!

My fascination was given a vision the day some old color video was restored. At one time the patriarch of the Ellzey family, Jack's dad, headed up a boys' camp in the summertime. Boys from across Texas would come to the ranch to experience a camp of exercise, good chow, creek fishing and swimming, and working a genuine cow-calf operation.

The video was from those camp days, and included shots of the remuda of some 30 horses that the ranch owned and the boys at camp used. In one particular scene I was delighted to see those horses being brought in from night pasture, and charging down off the caprock toward the corrals.

Dust was flying, heads were bobbing up and down, back and forth, and tails were streaming behind like rudders in the wind.

And there, just to the left in the video, came the wrangler, gently pushing and guiding what looked like a wild horse stampede in the daily routine of coming to work. I was told it was Jack. It looked as if he were riding on the sky! That never forgotten image prompted a poetic response many years later:

I could hear them long before I could see them

rumbling like thunder, rolling closer and loud.
Then, out of the sunrise they spilled over the caprock,
hooves pounding sod, manes dancing as the proud.

With brushstrokes of power and color they painted my heart!
And there, deftly directing that herd almost in flight,
rode the weathered wrangler, gliding with such ease
on that gifted black-white paint of marvel and delight.

As if of one accord, they came gracefully on, and I?
I was ensaddled with that horseman, riding on the sky!

I can still see that image at any moment by closing my
eyes, or by simply turning my face upward to the sky. I look
and there he is, and I am.

I wonder, does the sky hold such fascination for me
because of the image of Christ ascending there in His return
home? Is that indeed the vast depth from which He will one
day return?

I've tried to see the end of the sky before. I've stared
and gazed and imagined an ending point. While I long ago
learned that such childhood searching would come up without
fulfillment every time, now knowing there is apparently no end
to it all has simply expanded my amazement to equally endless
speculation and joy.

It's Incredible to me that a God capable of such endless
wonder and grace and compassion and mercy would make it
possible for us to imagine the unimaginable! How blessed we
are to know Him in the power and presence and wisdom and
courage of a Spirit of holiness and peace, here within, to guide
us upon our journey home.

When I think about such divine ways, I can only soar

with gratitude as I ride upon the sky every moment I remember that this is not all there is to it. Yet this is where my symphony is to be found and mixed and stirred!

"Riding on the Sky"
ACTS 1:6-11

"Why do you stand here and look up at an empty sky?" (Mssg)

I can only imagine what it must have been like for the disciples of Jesus, to have known Him both as Messiah and as Risen Lord, to have Him in hand, to lose Him in crucifixion, and to have Him in hand again, to watch as He ascended, left them for Home by rising into the sky, and then He was gone.

I'm not surprised that they were perhaps dumbfounded, watching in total awe as their Savior vanished into the depths without end! And I suspect that looking into the sky was never the same for them, ever again!

REFLECTIONS

When was the last time you just looked up, gazed into a sky more blue and deep than you could describe?

When was the last time you looked to see if you could find the end, the outer edge of the sky?

When you did, were you considering the possibility that Jesus might return to us by descending from those incomprehensible depths?

And have you ever been found by the Holy Spirit, gazing into the deep blue and been asked, "What are you looking for? Why are you staring into the empty sky?"

How has the Holy Spirit aided you in living this life to the fullest, keeping you focused on the call of God in hand, and blessed you to be a blessing in the here and now?

Has this focus in the moment kept you from remembering the depths of the sky and the promise therein?

Riding on the Sky

"Apple Dumping"

Matthew 28:20
"I'll be with you, daily, to the end of the end."

It's as if life could be an adventure planned in heaven, lived out in the laughter and tears of today, and reported upon with praise in our return home.

Such a claim is not always readily verifiable though. It was tough to see the morning that it was my turn to bring the horses in from the night pasture so we could get to our day's labor. I went to the corral where Apple had been kept through the night, cinched my saddle on him, and started to ride through the corral toward the horse pasture. I'd never ridden this handsome Appaloosa before, and I was glad to get a chance. In a flash and a snort, though, Apple burst into the air and I was flying instead of riding. I had been ejected and dumped by an Apple!

Now let me explain something. Apple is the gentlest horse I've ever worked with, maybe even capable of joining me on the conductor's podium! This is a horse that once rubbed his bridled face against the saddle shed door and got caught up, jerked his head away, and pulled that door off its hinges. Normally, and with any other horse on the ranch, a rodeo would have begun immediately. But Apple was so gentle that he stood perfectly still until the door, hanging from his bridle, was removed from his face!

This gentle horse had never before bucked anyone off – I was the first and last person to be dumped by this muscular 17-hands beauty! If that weren't enough, Tom's dad Lawrence saw it all as he came walking toward the corral. I didn't know that until I had collected myself from my high-soaring but short flight and heard him "busting a gut" with laughter!

When he got to me and found me okay, we both wondered what had happened, so we walked to the far end of the corral, straight up to a now calm and quiet Apple, and examined the situation. Quickly the boss saw the cause and said, "*I guess nobody told you Apple doesn't like a back cinch!*" Tom was in trouble.

As funny as that moment was then and is still now, the greater gift for me is that in the remembrance I can almost hear a strain of dissonant cello lines giving way to a very light-hearted symphonic dance led by trumpets and drums. For through that unexpected experience I found divine grace in the fact that neither Apple nor I was injured, and in my learning a much needed lesson about what Apple liked and did not like, or would not put up with.

In addition, I was given new insight into how privileged we humans are to have been enabled to gentle and train the amazing and beautiful and powerful horse for both our work and our pleasure. I sing praise to God for that cool morning with its unexpected flight of the Apple dumping, and brand new gratitude for how I found God present in the moment and now in the remembrance.

"Apple Dumping"
MATTHEW 28:20

In Many ways, the Messiah promises never to leave those who believe in Him. The promise is there in the companionship of the Holy Spirit. And the promise is incredibly simple to those who seek to live in His grace, teaching and loving with His compassion and mercy. He said, "*I will be with you . . . day after day after day!*" (Mssg)

To me, that means not only will that divine presence accompany us wherever we go; there won't be a single day that the Holy Spirit isn't available to guide and encourage, empower and teach, bless and multiply the work of the Savior in and through us.

When life throws us for a loop, or bucks us off, He is there, even if it happens day after day after day!

But as we accept the sensitivity of the Spirit as our own, it seems possible to me that when we're flying through the air, wondering how and/or when we're going to come down, even there – so far from solid ground or concrete understanding – if we look or listen or watch, we'll find Him there, riding the wind with us!

REFLECTIONS

None of us escapes the inevitable moment when, as life would have it, we are caught completely off guard by surprising circumstances or events that bumfoozle us. What happened? How did it happen? Why did this happen? What will the outcome be?

When was the last time you were absolutely and totally surprised by life and suddenly frightened by the unknown?

When did you last find yourself unseated from your expectations, needing to get up and dust off, and wondering what just happened?

How did you respond the last time life knocked the wind out of you, and as you struggled to catch your breath, as you came face to face with your faith?

Is it not true that if we trust the promise of God's presence to us, moment by moment, day after day after day, then we can learn to look first not for answers to those "why" questions, but to claim divine courage, wisdom, and grace as our own? In those divine gifts we are blessed with insight that may lead to different questions.

In the glory of your survival, what message would You have me share with my family and/or circle of influence?

You caught me in mid-air and revealed Your intimate concern and care of me: what words or actions might I take to illustrate this divine power to others?

How can I best express my gratitude, my joy, and my trust for Your catching me on the way down?

"Her name: Calypso"

Psalm 125:1-2; Proverbs 3:5-6
"Trust God from the gut, and God will lead you with clarity."

I was also challenged to express a hearty praise the day I was invited to be a part of the help with a roundup of steers on the M-Cross ranch. I didn't have to take a horse as our host John invited me to ride his 20-year old Arabian mare named Calypso. I was told that she was not real fast but that she was quick and surefooted, and that she could go all day long. John said I could trust her, so I trusted his word.

When we had gathered that Canadian River bottom pasture and headed the bunch for the house, a lone steer broke away. I was part of the drag and John signaled me to give chase and bring him back. That crazy critter had a good lead on us, but Calypso was fast enough to catch up over a quarter-mile stretch of ground. There, just as I was ready to nudge her into that steer's shoulder and turn him back, Calypso stumbled!

I am a living witness to the truth that in certain dynamic circumstances, a person can truly watch an entire life roll before the eyes of remembrance! In a flash, I saw it all, from a 5-year old building his first snow fort, to a giddy groom kissing his beautiful bride, through to a cowboy discovering a lone wildflower one fine Spring morning and being blessed with awe. It was all there, in that fleeting instant when I was certain both Calypso and I were headed for the hard dirt and not sure either of us would get up.

But she caught herself – she did not fall. And after I stepped off to scratch her face and hug her neck, and give us both a minute to stop shaking, I was relieved to discover an intimate respect for what had been claimed: you can trust her!

I can't begin to imagine now how my experience might feel or sound to the angels, how they might tremble with us as they vicariously face the unknown and in an instant recapture the known security of standing, though shaking, in gratitude for a trusted mare like Calypso.

Personally, I came through that roundup with the deeply affirmed assurance that no matter what may appear to be fact in this life, the truth is that God is present in each and every crisis and divine response, there to bless us with peace beyond our human understanding no matter the outcome.

I've grown to believe that while Calypso was indeed trustworthy, even more is God worthy of my trust. After all, if this life is in fact an adventure planned in Heaven, then Calypso deserves a minuet of her own!

"Her name: Calypso"
PSALM 125:1-2

Simply put, as solid and immovable as mountains seem to be, so is God even less movable! God is a hard "solid rock" of dependability. If we believe our lives are adventures planned in Heaven, we can depend on, trust, and love the God whose forgiveness, grace, mercy, compassion, wisdom, and courage are totally, absolutely immovable beyond our understanding!

PROVERBS 3:5-6

That immovable trustworthiness is offered to us by God's own voice as God sometimes whispers in our hearts and sometimes speaks clearly in our hearts of faith. We don't have to understand that voice either – we just need to trust what we're told, follow without fear, and discover each and every time that God's way is always, always right and good.

REFLECTIONS

Have you ever had one of those moments when you could swear you'd seen your whole life flash before your eyes in an instant?

How did you like the replay? Were you pleased with what you saw? Do you wish you could change anything there?

Do you trust God enough to take you from this very moment and begin leading you once again upon the pathway that leads Home?

Listen for God's sweet voice, trust without wavering from what you've been told, and you WILL find that God is worthy of your trust, and you WILL live this life as an adventure planned in Heaven. Then, when you get back home, you'll have plenty of grace reports to share with the angels awaiting your return!

Her Name: Calypso

5

"Windrider"

Psalm 23

"The Lord, The Lord Creator God, and none less, guides me all the way Home!"

As different as Apple and Calypso were from each other, so were the unique personalities of Chief, Sundown, Popeye, Whiskers, Buck, Happy, Blue, Murphy, Hot Tamale, Snips, Bubba, Dinny, and Joker. They came in a wide variety of breeds and sizes through the years, with different names and colors, and in my experience also with special gifts.

Chief, for example, was full of cow sense and so quick that he almost dropped me beside a barbed wire fence when he expertly anticipated the cut of a cow that decided to head back to where she came from! If I had been a quarter second slower reacting, I would have been picking Indian blanket out of my teeth while Chief finished the job of pushing that cow to the corral by himself.

Popeye had to have been part draft horse. His feet were dinner plates, and his neck was thick as a healthy young cottonwood. He was a bit rough in the trot, but being on him honed my riding technique and made me more responsive on

21

any mount. And when I needed to cut him loose, Popeye could open a full gallop that just floated over the terrain. It was as if I were gliding over a cushy carpet of buffalo grass!

While I'm not a roper, never was offered a lesson, and didn't particularly want one – I'd watched too many surprise rodeos – Happy was as good a roping horse as any I've watched. For any roper, green or experienced, Happy was stout and helpful, and if something on the end of a catch rope fought back, he hit an extra gear and pulled like a logging team. I never saw him lose a calf or a battle. He was also a pleasure for me in a rope free roundup!

Bubba was a lot like Popeye, without the gliding gallop. He was a strong and gentle utility horse. He could do lots of things well, though none perfectly. But he was dependable day in and day out.

Then there was Whiskers – a horse that I promise you looked as if he was walking in his sleep no matter what he was doing. Grazing, chasing cattle, or loping across a pasture, to watch him made one wonder when he was going to stop and lie down for a nap! In spite of the appearance, though, he was willing and athletic, and he would work all day long without complaining.

Maybe it's not what every cowboy dreams of, but to ride a horse with the combination of the best of those skills is fun to contemplate. To be cow smart, quick, strong, stubborn, gentle, and able to run as smoothly as a carpet: what a dream. I'd call such a horse Windrider myself.

Just as I find in my own life the presence of God's mighty rushing wind alive and well, present and comforting, challenging and gracious, forgiving and encouraging, so riding upon the Wind of faith does indeed lead me to green pastures and beside still waters.

To recall how I've been securely astride Windrider while wandering through dark valleys and finding myself safely delivered to the other side, refreshes my joy, and stirs God's glory and my gratitude from deep within.

I'd like to take an angel with me on a Windrider someday.

"Windrider"

PSALM 23

We all know the Psalm, or at least parts of it, by heart. We know how the Psalmist proclaimed that in the Lord, he had everything he could ever need; how he could trust the Lord to grant safe shelter, rest from labors and fears, protection from harm even when surrounded by darkness, and an over abundance of sustenance for the body.

We know that in the heart of that exclamation of honor to the Lord, in the security of the Lord's watch-care and provision, in the assurance of a safe return home forever, there 0resides the divine promise of sustenance for the spirit as well.

It's as if the Psalmist has ridden every different kind of horse, known every rough shod, bumpy, quick and jerky ride; it's as if he has known both dependable temperament and snorty temper, and found one, indeed found the Spirit of God to offer a ride that soothes and calms every possible anxiety or fear.

Could this have been the first ride upon the wind?

REFLECTION

Somewhere along the line in our young lives we learn to fear, we learn what hurts, we learn the difference between hot and cold, we find out what it's like to be hungry. Often we're too young to make a connection between those learning experiences and the presence and care of God.

As you grew older and faced those same challenges, when did you first recognize the presence of God there?

How often have you been satisfied to make God's love an adequate band aid for the wounds inflicted by life?

When did you first hear someone say that the Lord wants to provide more than a bandage, that He wants to provide total healing and wisdom as well?

When did you grow to a point in faith that you knew you were accepting so much less of what God wants you to have" When did you determine to live more fully in trust, enough trust to walk boldly through darkness and to step up to the table with complete thanksgiving as you shared in His feast?

Have you ever ridden on the wind of God's love?

6

"Marshmallow"

Deuteronomy 4:29-31
"No matter what, seek God, and you will not be abandoned."

I don't have anything against smaller animals like cats and dogs. Critters like skunks and raccoons and armadillos and snakes you can have. But dogs and cats are mostly okay, even though I'd rather not own one personally.

My preference is working with larger animals, specifically the horses and cattle on a ranch. I know no domesticated, trained, or herd animal is perfect. But I also know how much dynamite can be packaged in a dog no bigger than a large cantaloupe.

Take Drover for example. He was a small white mutt, the sidekick to a larger golden mutt named Sadie, and by far the lesser in courage on the LZ ranch, at least in my view. Drover was mostly a follower and shied out of the way of cattle long before they could have been any danger to him. I guess that's part of the reason I took to calling him Marshmallow: all white, a bit fluffy, and pretty much full of hot air as good cow dogs go.

But he sure stirred up a pasture-load of trouble the day Tom and I tried to bring in cattle in "the home place" for feeding. It was mid-Spring, and we weren't sure we could do it, but we decided to try and call the pasture of newly bought steers in with the pickup horn they'd been called with to their feed all Winter.

We were pleasantly surprised when it seemed to be working. The steers, all 80 of them, were a bit timid because we wanted to call them into the front lot, which would save us the trouble of rounding them up later. They were headed that way. The pickup was into the lot, and about half the herd was through the gate.

Suddenly there came a sickly "yip" from under the bottom board of an adjoining corral. It was Drover, Marshmallow, trying to act tough from behind protective cover. All cowboy hell broke loose!

Before we could do anything halfway constructive, the steers spooked and split down the middle. Half of the now crazy critters blew north, took out two fences around the hay lot, and didn't stop running for a full mile. The other half seemed to scamper backward for fifty yards before turning and disappearing to the far back side of the home pasture.

Then it was all over but the screaming. Tom was so mad his red face could have lit up a midnight moonless sky like a bonfire, and Marshmallow disappeared down the creek, not to be seen for close to three days. For a stupid move and sad little yip, being gone for that long was pretty smart. Drover allowed time for things to cool down a bit before he, tail between the legs, came whimpering back to the house looking for some sympathy and supper.

That afternoon was spent hunting down and gathering

42 steers in the home pasture. The next day we started the search for the other 38 head. All told, we repaired three fences, doctored four calf-hide barbed wire wounds, and lost a whole day out of the week's work plan.

But that was it. Everything was fixable and forgivable, and the groaning gave way to laughter. The day was not destroyed! Lost hours were adjusted into next week, and life rolled back into routine until the next ranch rodeo.

Life's crazy like that, though. When everything seems smooth as silk, such peaceable reverie can be blown to bits with sudden impact. The news of someone you love graduating from this journey across the stage to our Heavenly home, a fall that breaks an arm, a dead battery in the pickup when you're already late, all these and many other surprises can catch you off guard.

And yet, perhaps in those moments especially, our Father God is intimately present to us, ready to offer relief and reassurance, grace and gentleness, as well as the steady reminder that we're never alone.

In moments like that, when we may feel abandoned or helpless or confused or angry, we are offered the blessed assurance that this is not all there is to it, and the sweet invitation to consider how a blasted but now humorous experience with a Marshmallow mutt might become a cherished story about the glory of God in the midst of surprise!

"Marshmallow"
DEUTERONOMY 4:29-31

One of the most cherished promises of the Lord is found here. It's a promise, an assurance, that no matter how deep the mud might be we're stuck in, no matter how hot the heat that tries to roast us, no matter how forsaken we may at times feel, if, IF we choose to seek the face of our Lord with all our heart, with everything in us that can conceive of and pursue him, *we will find him!*

Not only that, we can cling to that divine promise because this, our Creator God, is merciful, is in total unabashed love with us, and he *will not* abandon us, leave us to our own resources, let us fall farther than he can reach out to catch us . . . IF we seek him with all our heart!

REFLECTION

When was the last time you had done everything you thought you had been asked to do, everything you needed to do to complete your task/work with integrity and satisfaction, only to have it all blown away at the last moment by a hurtful word from a co-worker or boss, or an accident that completely discombobulated your efforts? And, how did you handle it?

What is the standard of success that guides your efforts in faith and trust? Is that the same standard that guides you in your family and/or job?

Have you ever been guilty of a negative attitude, or body language that speaks volumes about your displeasure and after making that offering found that it was totally uncalled for, unnecessary, and/or deeply disappointing to a spouse, child, co-worker or friend?

When was the last time part or all of the above transpired, and how long did it take for you to remember that IF you seek the Lord, his divine mercy will bless you with a capacity for forgiveness, for gentleness, with eyes capable of seeing his grace in the midst of it all?

It's not easy to compile a grace report in the midst of

turmoil or upheaval, but could those times be perhaps the richest opportunities for mining such grace?

Marshmallow

"Stumble Weeds and Flats"

Zechariah 10:9
"No matter how far you are from Home, remember the Lord your God."

Not all ranch rodeos are animal created. One early winter morning, with the season's first dusting of snow all over everything, I took the flatbed pickup across the creek to check on a small herd of mama cows and late season calves. They were smart enough to be huddled under the cap rock, out of the north breeze blowing cold across the ranch.

I unloaded alfalfa for them, counted to make sure they were all present for breakfast, and rolled back toward the house. I was the only one at the Lower Section that morning. Others were in town or out of town and I was enjoying the melting quiet.

As I pointed the flatbed back toward the house, though, I heard a soft thump and wondered if I had picked something up crossing the creek. I stopped to check things out and found the back right tire dead flat.

The natural thing to do was to pull the pickup seat forward and get the jack out so the tire could be changed. I did that, then pulled the spare off the bed of the pickup and as I maneuvered to put the spare where the flat had been I discovered that this particular spare didn't fit this particular pickup! It was the right size tire, but wrong wheel.

My options were slim and none. I had no choice but to walk back to the shed alongside the house and find the right spare and then bring it back, which I planned to do in the blue pickup at the house. So I started toward the house, only about three quarters of a mile west of my flat. No problem, I thought! But I quickly found myself fighting through some tall freeze-killed and wet weeds that acted more like bear traps than ground cover.

I picked my feet up higher and higher as I trudged along, deciding to march my way straight over the mess instead of making the walk twice as long by going around. My mistake! Halfway to the house I got a bit lazy, or overconfident, and tried to trudge instead of March, and it cost me. My foot found one of those traps to be stronger than my tiring legs and I tripped, fell flat forward, and ate weed spiced snow before I could brace my fall.

Getting up was a challenge, but once accomplished I vowed to march, and finally made it to the shed. Leaning next to the front bumper on the blue pickup, there was my spare, sadly and mistakenly switched with the spare on the flatbed. Thankfully, it was aired up, so all I had to do was get it back to the flatbed. Sadly, the left rear tire on the blue pickup was also dead flat, and the spare was way out there leaning against the flatbed!

Walking out from under the shed I caught a glimpse of the riding mower. I wondered if I might get that thing started and enjoy an easier return. Then I examined the mower and found a flat tire on the front. A quick trip to the tool shed uncovered an air tank, but a busted hose kept me from using the compressor to fill it. There was no way to air up the mower tire, so my choice was simple: roll the spare back through the middle of the bear trap ground, or roll it back the long way around.

I made my choice: I thought I'd roll the spare in front of me and let it smash out a trail I could walk in with ease! Silly me. Before the spare and I got back to the flatbed I tasted snow again.

Finally, the flat was changed and I made my way back to the house. By that time I was also hungry so a late morning snack was in order. While I was munching on toast covered in peanut butter and honey it occurred to me that this was the best flavored snack I'd eaten in a very long time.

Could it be, could it just possibly be that the morning trials, the challenge of the flat to change, and the taste of weed spiced snow, had blessed me with a divine appreciation for the snack in hand? I'd never appreciated a snack like this one so much. Could it possibly be a Heaven-gift to recognize that salty sweet and crunch as a reminder of God's presence even amidst the stumble weeds and flats?

Listen, human and angel audience alike: nothing tastes better than the sweet reminder that God is ever present and blessing all the way home, no matter the level of difficulty discovered upon the pathways we choose!

"Stumble Weeds and Flats"
ZECHARIAH 10:9

The people had been scattered from horizon to horizon, with the promise that they would raise their families and then return. But in the mean time, the times could seem pretty mean! However, as mean as it might seem such a far distance from home, the people always remembered their God.

REFLECTION

At times even right choices can seem to be wrong, because of the difficulties that go with them. When did you last make what you believed to be a right choice and found yourself tripping and falling flat?

Sure, most of us wish the journey home could be paved with smooth concrete, void of potholes, and covered quickly in a brand new pickup. But we all know that even when we get those rare kinds of moments, that's what they are: rare moments. So, where do you find your courage in those more common times of struggle along the bumpy road home?

On this particular ranch it was often true that "If it's not one thing, it's a hundred others!" Our typical response was frequently, "If all else fails, get a bigger hammer!" How do you handle it when you need, and maybe even find a bigger hammer, but know that's not the right response to the hundred other challenges? What method does the Lord use to soften you when necessary?

God's children are scattered to all parts of the earth. Each one is invited to return home to Him. In view of the crooked, tangled weed pathway before you, how's your journey progressing?

8

"Pickin' the Right Saddle"

Galatians 3:1-4a
"Choose the more trustworthy: law, or Christ?"

It's funny to me, how much we assume to be true until something proves our assumptions to be flawed if not outright wrong. I mean, when I was a kid in the saddle I didn't wonder about whether or not there were different kinds of saddles. I simply rode the saddle that was strapped on my horse for me.

Not until many years later, when I was older and wiser, did my ignorance begin to show through. Not until I rode a saddle with a high cantle and a shorter seat did it occur to me that saddles could be made to fit a cowboy's needs and makeup.

Sure, I'd seen those odd looking saddles that I was never invited to ride, like the old bucking saddle the LZs had tied up to the shed rafters. The seat was deep, the cantle was high, and the pommel was wide enough to hold most anything in tight.

And there was the old bulldogging saddle I saw in the local Museum of the Plains, with a low cantle and practically no pommel at all, so cowboys could slide out easier.

Time also helped me learn that a saddle could actually be handmade to suit a cowboy's preferences, each part measured, cut and built to specific specifications. But it wasn't until I went shopping for some new jeans in a western store, where they also had a couple hundred saddles on display that it dawned on me that I could find and buy a saddle to my own liking.

There, blessed with the distinctive smells of new leather as I walked in, I lost all awareness of jeans needs, and wandered in amazement among the seemingly endless choices that could be made. And there, after pulling a dozen or so saddles onto the test rack, I sat, and sat, and sat again, until I felt more comfortable in a saddle than I ever had before!

I guess that friends, and those who were willing to invite me to work with them, always had a shed full of their own saddles and I never needed to consider purchasing my own. But that day everything changed, and I spent my jeans money and more for the saddle I still ride today.

It made me laugh out loud the first time I saddled Dude with that new saddle and rode out into a pasture. My good friend Bobby and I had gone to the M-Cross Ranch to find and separate four or five bulls from a herd of mama cows. We were out there for several hours, sometimes loping long distances across a draw to fetch a lone bull, at other times moving at a leisurely pace through the herd. At one point it even took both of us to find, separate, and convince a bull from the midst of the ladies that our will was stronger than his, so we cut and chased and cut and chased again, until he was convinced and walking toward the corral.

Needless to say, we, and our horses, got a good

workout as we faced and finished the job. Afterward, as I stepped down off Dude, it was as if I'd never been in the saddle – at least not in any of the other saddles I'd borrowed that didn't fit me, that had lower cantles than I knew I preferred, that were longer than I needed.

Honestly, from that experience I learned how comfortable it could be to ride most of a day and get down without those aches, stresses and saddle sores I was expecting!

Funny, how in that one day I learned so much about how important it was to pick the right saddle! But the experience was not wasted on me. I take care of that saddle like the treasure it is when I'm in it. And I do so in part because the right saddle helps me concentrate more easily on the job we're doing, instead of carrying a concern about whether I can stay in it, or how sore I might be when I'm done with an ill-suited saddle.

Such saddle lessons are easier learned than others life lessons. I'm grateful that as tough as it can be, it grows easier day by day to trust the Holy Spirit. It saddens me that I've been so stubborn! But I'm delighted that I've learned, through varied experiences, that the Spirit of the Living God in me is indeed and always worthy of my total trust.

"Pickin' the Right Saddle"
GALATIANS 3:1-4a

The young believers of Galatia had apparently taken leave of their senses! They were acting as though they couldn't remember who the Savior was! For some reason, they apparently thought they could finish the work laid out before them by God without including God in the work! They were in the wrong saddle for the job at hand.

REFLECTION

When I was a boy I thought like a boy, I looked like a boy, I acted like a boy, and was a long way from being the real cowboy I dreamed about being! If I had had my own way, I would have become a real cowboy overnight, by magically awakening to find myself on Trigger, and fully equipped with experience, wisdom, and talent for the work at hand. How often have you found a personal dream to have come true without doing the hard labor of commitment and patience?

At one point in my ranch work the boss was firmly entrenched again the purchase and use of a 4-wheel drive pickup. His feeling was that any work we couldn't do with a conventional 2-wheel drive unit was work we didn't need to do anyway! Then in about 1977 or so the snows were heavy, there were several hundred feeder steers on the flats to take care of, and his conventional pickups kept getting stuck in the snow and mud. After having been pulled out several times by a kindly neighbor *with a 4-wheel drive unit,* he decided to try one on his ranch! He was in the wrong saddle for a long time, before relenting and riding something new. How stubborn are you when in comes to making changes in old ways?

Sometimes we don't know we have choices. Ignorance can be bliss, I suppose, but when I discovered the possibility of owning and riding in a saddle that fit me and my work, it was liberating. As it was, I stumbled onto the possibility. Other than cowboy luck, where do you go when looking for truth, particularly truth for right living?

"A Winter Lament"

Romans 5:1-5

"Our peace grows through trust, and hope is ours as the Spirit's gift."

There is no doubt that in my cowboy experience I've been invited, day after day, to either buckle or grow under the pressures exerted by surprise circumstances, or Mother Nature, or a cranky old cow, or the fact that the sun came up way before my tired body was ready to rise with it.

Such was the case in the winter of '77. For me it seemed like the coldest winter I'd ever experienced, in part because it was my first winter as a full-time hand on the LZ ranch spending frozen hours in the out of doors. Much of what we did that winter was new to me, so much different than those days when as a young boy I purely loved everything that had to do with ranch life and work.

These were days when profits were to be made by seeing yearlings through the winter on wheat pasture, and the more the better. So daily one of us had to drive up out of Wolf Creek to the flats, stop by a county pump station and fill a humongous water trailer, and then delivers water to different pastures checking and filling and breaking ice on water troughs and tanks.

While one among us was at that solitary and mostly windy-frozen task, another would take a 4-wheel drive pickup into the creek pastures and check windmills and tanks there.

Both jobs were difficult to say the least. But the part of the challenge that helped make it bearable was that Tom and I were both into weight lifting at the time, and we had visions of looking like Conan the Barbarian in pursuit of Red Sonja the Warrior Queen.

So while we might not have enjoyed the frozen tundra and skin-freezing wind, we didn't necessarily mind breaking ice on those tanks.

In fact, Tom got even a bit impatient with trying to do that job with a 5 or 6-pound axe. So one evening we went to the machine shed, he pulled out the welder and some scrap iron, and set about building a homemade ice axe, fashioned in a way that was supposed to direct the ice away from the cowboy as it busted up the ice as if it'd been hit with TNT, and heavy enough that what might take ten blows with an ordinary axe could be accomplished in fewer than half the blows.

As fit as we felt we were, the new ice axe was a delight to wield. We heaved the heavy 14-pounder overhead and slammed it down on the ice. The ice exploded as though facing the wrath of a barbaric, monstrous, muscular cowboy to be feared by man, woman, and bovine beast alike!

Thankfully, he was kind enough to share that homemade ice bomber, and it was in my hands on the coldest day of that winter. As I remember it, the high temperature was to reach only about ten above freezing, and in the midst of a stretch of a couple of weeks that didn't see the magical 32-degree mark. Obviously, the ice on those water tanks was thick and hard, making our job one that surely only such a barbarian could accomplish with efficiency.

As I approached the first tank on the ranch that morning, I was full of warm coffee and mystical dreams about exploding ice. My first swing with that ice buster came down with authority and certainty, and it glanced off awkwardly as if I'd tried to bust concrete with it. Not to be denied, though, I raised it again and again, and finally I could sense that the next blow would open the tank up to water.

I swung with all the strength I had, and sure enough, the ice gave way, and the axe crashed into the icy water below, and unlike what we had planned, my whole front side was covered with that freezing water – my face, my coat, my chaps, my jeans, and my boots! Almost instantly I was a walking icicle as the wind froze me stiff before I could reach the warmth of the pickup!

Sitting there trying to thaw, on the one hand proud of my accomplishment and on the other groaning at the challenge, I remembered, one tank down, nine stops yet to make.

What a journey that day proved to be! Moving from tank to tank, freezing and thawing, freezing and thawing, acting like an ice-mashing maniac, and then bragging to Tom about my escapades at the supper table – what a day that proved to be!

What it proved, if nothing else, was the truth of the words of the Apostle Paul, words that rang through the sounds of shattering ice and encouraged me from tank to tank, that while it's true in life it's also true in faith: suffering develops endurance, endurance develops character, and character develops hope.

Indeed, this character developed a hope for the end of the day, birthed in the endurance of that arctic suffering! And now I get to share with the angels that in remembering the blessings of God no matter the challenges at hand, how warm it truly is inside, in the spirit, no matter how cold it can be outside in the winter.

"A Winter Lament"
ROMANS 5:1-5

Patience? I prayed for patience once, then bragged about it to my youth sponsor who said, "O, honey, you don't know what you've asked for!" Mercy was she ever right! I prayed for patience with my little sisters, and what I got was a fire-storm of opportunities to be patient as they pestered and hounded me without mercy.

Then we grew up, from kids to young adults, and finally to qualified adults who have assumed responsibility for their personal lot in life. And low and behold, here we are, groomed through the patience we later discovered that we all prayed for, to live life with passionate expectancy! What's God got in store for us now?

REFLECTION

Patience may be perhaps the hardest lesson for someone in our modern culture to learn. That's so in part because we seem to be bombarded with commercialism and greed that demands we consider not what we need, but rather what we ought to possess, to have. Life feels as if it has little meaning apart from the accumulation of "stuff" that in and of itself holds little value as life-building tools.

Such a culture speaks little of patience, or of virtue, or of anticipation. "Passionate expectancy" may hold no more meaning or intriguing invitation than the prospect of attaining *autarkeia.* When you don't know the language, you don't know what the offer is? And whose got the time to look it up, or learn the language?

Could you ever define your life, or parts of it, as a proverbial rat race?

What do you look forward to from day to day?

It seems to me that "passionate expectancy" is a divine concept or possibility. Do you hold any such expectancy in your daily journey?

It's possible that only in experiencing the joy of such "passionate expectancy" can one actually come to know *autarkeia* in this life. Is it possible that only in living life in a divine expectancy of what God's going to do next in your life can you know a measure of divine *contentment?*

A Winter Lament

"Beyond the Mist"

James 4:13-15
"You are like a surprising mist that also vanishes just as surprisingly."

I could barely believe it when Tom told me we were still going. We were set to head north to Beaver County in Oklahoma, up to the Prairie Parthenon, a ranch home built with columns and an inner courtyard, kind of a miniature Roman palace.

We were part of a three-state crew there to gather four-section pastures of a cow-calf operation. The herd was being sold and shipped, today, in spite of the dense morning misty fog that lay across the prairie like a blanket wet enough to drink.

Tom and I had fed and watered two horses apiece, saddled one, loaded all four for the trip, and he assured me the fog would lift by the time we hit the Sooner state line.

It didn't. But we forged ahead, as did the whole crew, and we were mounted and in the first pasture by eight o'clock. We were instructed to move slowly so as not to miss a single animal, especially baby calves, and to move everything toward the southeast corner of the pasture. I was sent down the west fence line to ride south and watch specifically for a couple of bulls that had been seen out that way last night.

Only a hundred yards from the catch-pens I was glad to have been told to move slowly simply because the sage brush and sand hills presented a challenge beyond what we were used to on the LZ place. There the solid ground rolled along the creek with draws and yucca to contend with, while here the ground itself was a soft sweat maker, and the sage was thicker and more abundant than our Texas cactus. It quickly became clear to me why we had brought extra horses – one for the morning, the other for the afternoon.

About a half mile down the fence those two bulls appeared out of the mist, spotted me and Deuce, and took off south like a couple of frightened 1,800 pound deer! The sand and sage didn't slow them in the least, and my hope was that while I wasn't trying to drive them since they were headed in the right direction, Deuce and I could bend them a bit east so they wouldn't plow through the fence a mile and half away.

In truth, those crazy bulls were outrunning us, so my job turned into a race over unfamiliar ground, knowing full well these graceful behemoths could jump that south fence if they wanted to!

Believe it or not, as Deuce did a masterful job of dodging and jumping and moving like I'd never asked him to do before, I fell into his rhythm and flew with him in spite of the obvious possibilities for taking a tumble together. We managed to bend the track of the bulls, to join the herd in the corner, and to bring two bulls too tired to run any more along for the mostly smooth move back north to the catch pens.

The rest of the day included an incredibly delicious

lunch in the Parthenon, the roundup and loading of another huge pasture, and a mist that persisted until it came time for us to motor back to Texas.

Tom and I didn't talk much on the way home. We were bushed and traveled mostly in comfortable silence, which gave me time to consider what we'd just been through.

Out of the mist was born in me a renewed gratitude for the physical capabilities of a good horse, an awe at how animals as large as those bulls could move so gracefully and quickly, and a revived appreciation for how I had been blessed of God to spend the day doing something I truly enjoy, being a cowboy.

The work is mostly very hard and almost daily smelly and dirty. Horses and cattle don't always want to cooperate. And usually it has to be done no matter what Mother Nature offers with the rising sun each morning. Perhaps that's why so few people are willing to do that, to be cowboys and cowgirls!

And perhaps that's the reportable news I'll share with the angels: beyond the mist comes surprises of joy and gratitude and fulfillment in a job done well.

"Beyond the Mist"
JAMES 4:13-15

It's amazing how a little mist, or fog, can transform any occasion. Sometimes those occasions can blind us to the way of God, can cause us to believe life is all about us and our desires, and become potentially deadly. At other times such a shroud can cause us to focus on the present moment in new and renewing ways. A fog or mist that can lead us astray might also lead us to the Lord.

REFLECTION

I didn't see how we could do the work, literally! The mist was so dense we could barely see, and yet, persistence and patience paid off as the job in hand was accomplished in spite of the unusual visual challenge of the day. We could have been distracted, but as it turned out we were caused to focus. When was the last time an unusual circumstance presented itself to your life? Be it a family challenges, a lame horse, or weather conditions, did you pack it in and forget about moving forward, or did the challenge simply force you to focus, and in turn aid you in getting through to completion?

There have been times in my life when I dreamed about my tomorrows. And while that in itself is not bad, it can become unhealthy if dreaming blinds me to the realities of the day in hand. A good foggy day has always blessed me with a forced means of focus. And occasionally that focus has blessed me with divine insight, with a vision for things I might have missed if I were simply dreaming way out in front of the day. When was the last time circumstance gave you a chance to focus like that? Did it anger or distress you, or did it liberate you to see anew the blessings of God's presence in the moment?

"Hoots"

Proverbs 18:24
"Some friends, not all, stick with you as close as family."

I don't remember how many times we stopped in at Hoot's, but I remember those days with clarity. We'd go up onto the flats to lay out or roll up electric fence, to haul in or haul out a wheat-pasture full of yearlings, to water or doctor those calves.

It always amazed me how often Tom could time the work so that getting done happened right about noon.

It was then and there, noontime on the flats, we'd roll into town and stop for lunch. And as far as we were concerned there was only one place for us to stop: Hoots.

That was the name of the owner-operator-cooks: Hoots. Mercy could they do just that – own, operate and cook up the finest foods in town. It didn't matter if it was just a burger or grilled cheese, a steak or breakfast; it came to the table piping hot, seasoned perfectly, and tasty all the way down.

But the best part of those noon meals was the dessert. Delectable and amazing pies and cakes were filled with sweet delight, and we claimed that dessert was the one ingredient in the meal we needed in order to make it through the afternoon. My favorite was that magnificent, thick, hot and tangy cherry pie, with homemade vanilla ice cream on top. I don't know what the magic ingredient was, but it was like no other cherry pie I'd ever eaten, or yet eaten today. There was a masterful blend of tart and sweet, with a tiny twist of tantalizing difference I couldn't identify, and Mrs. Hoots wouldn't divulge her secret!

It wasn't unusual that we'd walk out of that place a bit overstuffed, but not a bit guilty because we were well aware that it'd be worked off by supper time.

As much as I'd like to believe that cuisine was glorious, I know better. The food was indeed special, but the glory in those meals was the friendship we shared with the Hoots, with others stuffed into those tiny booths or at the bar stools, and between us, Tom and me.

Maybe it was so special for me because I've never been perfectly sure or assured that I really was or am a real cowboy. Yes, I've been bucked out of a saddle, stomped on and kicked by all manner of mangy bovine, more often than I like to confess fallen flat on my rear in fresh piles of fertilizer, and sometimes all in less than a day! But as the son of a band director and English teacher, my bloodline doesn't qualify.

So maybe being an officially accepted genetically birthed cowboy chowin' down in Hoots for the entire world to see was only the vehicle through which I can today claim: I have a lifetime friend in Tom.

Yes, these intervening years have seen us both venture far and wide away from, back to, and away from the ranch again, each of us going separate ways. But I relish the confidence that if Hoots was still open, we could go there anytime, together, and pick up the conversation right where we left if off the last time we were there.

My, what a blessed thought! To know a friend who will always be a friend in part because we've been through the rain and the sunshine, the sweat and the fertilizer of life, the Hoots pie and the ranch cookout hotdogs together: this is a divine gift I cherish with him, and with many others in whose company I've ridden. It's a gift: true friendship, for which I offer the joy of God's glory both today and forever.

"Hoots"
PROVERBS 18:24

I'd had many "friends" in my young life, and Mike was one of them. He was, that is, until that summer morning that, for reasons long forgotten, we got into a tussle. We ended up wrestling each other to the ground, his teeth braces cut his gums, and bleeding and angry, he got up and stomped off down the street, around the corner, and I sadly thought gone forever.

That is, until later, toward noon. Ray and I were in the backyard roasting wieners on Dad's grill when Mike came through the back gate! No longer bleeding, and neither of us able to remember why we tangled, he and Ray and I indulged in hot dogs until the package was gone!

That day was another indication of what we were: friends. Sure we tussled a time or two – all boys do, it seems. But those scrapes along the way didn't keep us from knowing we could depend on each other like brothers! We were, and are, friends.

REFLECTION

Like my relationship with Tom, Mike and I also knew

what it meant to be able to depend on one another, sometimes at the oddest of hours.

Is it just a miracle of happenstance? Is the nature of close-knit shared experiences? Is it dumb luck?

How hard does a person have to work to cultivate, nourish and sustain a true friendship with one who sticks by you like family?

I trust that the Lord is master of familial relationships and thank God daily for the gifts of friendship.

"Christmas NUTS"

1 Corinthians 1:3-9
"God IS faithful – never underestimate the Spirit."

I've lived all my life in Kansas, Oklahoma and Texas, with most of it on the High Plains, and particularly in the Texas Panhandle. I've also spent many weeks vacationing in Colorado and New Mexico. I know something of what high humidity is like from the deep south in Texas, the southeast corner of Kansas, and the heart of Oklahoma. And I know something about the higher and dryer climates of the High Plains and Rocky Mountains.

I speak with a bit of authority when I make reference to my widely different experiences in the winters of those places. The cold of the Rockies is, for example, big as the mountains different from the loaded with humidity cold down around Houston. The dry cold is simply much different from the humid cold, but cold is still cold.

It was on one of those bitterly cold days in the Texas Panhandle that I had to be out and about just a day or two before Christmas. A couple of breachy steers were discovered on a neighbor's home pasture, I had used the pickup to push them back into the place they came from, and I was doing one of those jobs I truly enjoy: walking and inspecting and fixing fence.

As I looked for the place where those two wayfaring steers might have crawled through, or over, broken or loose wires, I walked a couple of miles through creek breaks. The morning was still and silent except for the hauling of my overboots through the dry grass and a shallow skiff of snow.

The pleasures of that solitude were heightened by the freezing temperatures that might have penetrated my winter wear if not for the warming exercise of walking and tugging on wire and pounding staples.

I paused in the midst of the labors several times to watch a bird gently alight on a fallen tree branch, examine the safety of the setting, and then hop down to the creek and quench its thirst; to watch in amazement at the grace of the deer that I'd spooked up as she disappeared into a plum thicket for cover; and to linger long enough to gaze deeply into the clear blue sky overhead.

There was no doubt in my mind that the first Christmas was as far different from those moments as it was different in location and century. But the beauty witnessed in the pauses of that day was no less sacred to me as I remembered the celebration to come.

Christmas through the years had blossomed in my spirit, as it does for most that grow from childhood joy to adult awe in the true gifts of God. It had come to represent my personal invitation from the Creator to recognize that what I could sense as a human was little of nothing compared to the endless expanse of creation. It came to represent a divine love that invited me home! And it came to represent the possibility that I am, and we are not alone in this journey.

My morning meditations were drawn even higher as I finished the fence walk and crossed the creek at the Dutcher place. White smoke was spiraling from the chimney of the house revealing warmth inside. Just as I turned to head for the pickup my friend Bill appeared on the porch and invited me in for tea.

It was an invitation warmly offered and gladly accepted. The change in temperature in the house was a shock to my face and quickly thawed what I didn't know was almost frozen! Then the steamy peppermint herb tea did the same work inside my skin, and the sugared pecans were tasty and energizing.

But what warmed and fed me most was Bill's Christmas tree. It was surprising and delightful to find, perched on a low table, the tallest, fullest tumble weed I'd ever seen, reaching to the ceiling. Upon its fragile branches were placed and hung strings of popcorn and dainty ornaments that looked to be antique.

Our conversation was simple as always and the comfort of the company was enriching. We were serenaded by the recording of a master guitarist floating through his own arrangements of Christmas carols.

Outside it was a high plains cold morning. But inside Bill's home, and my spirit, it was as warm as the Christmas season has ever been.

It was Christmas NUTS that nourish me still today: Never Underestimate the Spirit's power and desire to bless no matter what any given day might appear to hold forth in its beginnings. A cold walk along the creek birthed observations of divine life, remembrances of a journey home offered and chosen, and a reminder that in the gift of Christmas was born a Way-shower who is and always will be attentive and present to every traveler along the way.

In fact, it seems quite possible to me that Christmas may indeed be the first part of God's answer to our question, "How do we get home?"

So often we make choices that cloud our remembering who and whose we are and those choices throw us off the path that leads home. We seem to struggle with truly understanding who the Trail Boss, the Foreman, or the Source of direction is intended to be for us.

God's answer for me began with a divine invitation to make that journey home with Jesus, who was sent to us as a Way-shower because God wants us home as badly as we want to return!

So I say NUTS: Never Underestimate The Spirit! Therein is power to gain our attention, and to redirect us if need be so that our journey might remain true, even if not without days of snow kissed labors on behalf of a couple of stubborn steers.

"Christmas NUTS"
PSALM 22:31

It's a signed and sealed promise, a divine promise, a promise of God Almighty!
Even babies know before they're born, "God does what He says He's going to do!" There is no place in the promise to doubt, to fear, to wonder or speculate. This one is in concrete: if He said it, He's going to do it!

1 CORINTHIANS 1:3-9

Imagine: as much as we think we need, we often fail to note that in Christ we've got it all! We've got redemption's freedom, wisdom, and courage for the journey home, AND the companionship of the Christ who will "never give up on us!" This being so, it seems only wise that we Never Underestimate The Spirit's creative genius and love as we are guided with grace along the way home.

Never, ever, ever underestimate the Spirit. NEVER!

REFLECTION

What Christmas do you remember most vividly, and why?

And what birthday, Easter, swimming party, hug do you remember most, and why?

Is there a common thread within those things we remember most vividly? I suspect that those experiences that impact us the most are those that either blow us away with anger or fear, or those that draw us together with love, compassion, mercy, and joy. Of those experiences you remember most vividly, that bring you joy in the remembrance, could that joy be attributed to the companionship of the Holy Spirit, even if you didn't recognize it at the time?

13

"I'll Fly Away"

Psalm 55:6-8
"If I but had wings I could fly away to a restful safe haven."

A pastor friend of mine once said, "To what end, this faith? To know, to experience, to share the character of God in every aspect of life!"

It's been wondrous for me to find that his words hold true in so many aspects of ranch life. For instance, who would ever have thought the character of God might be found in the sweat-drenched hay field on a blazing hot Sunday in July?

Maybe the most demanding physical labor that I have ever faced was the work it took to bring in the hay off that 30-acre patch of alfalfa on the LZ ranch. We tried to get four cuttings each summer, and while we worked ourselves into better and better shape as the season progressed, it was always demanding labor.

Some of it was actually quite pleasant. If you happened to be the one cutting the hay by moonlight, the sweet smell of the ripe crop was almost intoxicating. It was like drifting through honeysuckle in the coolest part of the day!

Raking what had been cut was another matter. Timing was critical. There had to be enough moisture in the air to help keep the leaf on the stem, but it had to be dry enough that the hay would not self-ignite when packed into a tight bale.

Then there was the bailing, on a weathered older bailer that demanded almost as much time for upkeep and repair as it offered in actual bales of hay. At one point Tom was using a regular hammer to peck away at a bolt that had broken and was lodged between two feeder arms. It was then I heard him say for the first time, but certainly not the last, as he reached for a sledge hammer, "If all else fails, get a bigger hammer!"

None of this was beyond bearing, though. It was the stacking, the loading, and stacking, and unloading, and stacking again, moving those bails of 60 to 90 pounds each, and not knowing which they were until you put your back into lifting them, that wore a person out. Top that with the sweltering heat that threatened to melt a body away and the work was grueling.

Maybe that's why one summer we somehow found the unique combination that was used to re-hydrate and encourage us between loads. The first load in the heat of the afternoon sent us to the frig for a Gatorade and a Coors! Yup, the Gatorade was the re-hydration part, and the Coors was the re-courage part that made it possible to go back for yet another load!

That discovery fostered a poetic response:

Breakfast finished by 6
we're in the field loading alfalfa
      (weighing from 60 to 90 pounds a bail:
      the baler is spastically creaky!)
by 7, in plenty of time to witness

the last changing sky colors of sunrise.

Muscles loosen slowly, much slower than the pace
of the work, and we're swimming in sweat by 8.
Though too early begun, morning progresses
without a hay-rodeo or wreck
       (The straw-boss only falls off the truck
       in the afternoons!)
and noontime's lunch is welcome and tasty.

Work in the heat of the afternoon is
gruesome, and bodies weaken rapidly,
       (Straw-boss fell!)
but break time and its promise of the creek
and a quick skinny-dip keeps us pushing,
stacking and panting ahead.

After the cooling dip
we gather in the cottonwood shade of the yard
and straw-boss's wife brings
a gift of cold green Gatorade.

Now is the time for bolstering strength and resolve,
preparing for evening's final steamy hours,
and courage is ours when straw-boss
returns from a trip to the frig and we lustily warn:
"Look out Gatorade – here comes the Coors!"

Not being one who ever really liked beer, I usually
ended up with a Gatorade in each hand, while certain other
unnamed cowboys among us would fist a Coors in each hand.
Still, the combination seemed to work for us that day!

Thankfully, that beverage combination didn't much
affect or effect our faith while hauling hay. Busted knuckles

from baler repair, cheeks rotted from too many sunflower seeds eaten while trying to stay awake at the moonlight mowing, and chasing an occasional snake from underfoot could make you question your religion at times.

However, all that being true, I'll never forget the Sunday we had to work the hay because of the threat of hay-rotting rains to come.

It was about midway through the day, just before lunch break as I recall, and we were loading the sideless old wheat truck bed with bales of hay stacked as high as we dared. Tom's sister Jill was driving the truck while John from the M-Cross joined us for this particular cutting.

Somewhere along the way it was suggested that we honor the day with our own brand of church. As I recall it was John who led the singing, I offered up the prayers, and Tom was tagged with the preaching responsibilities.

While I don't remember a word of my prayers, or a word of Tom's sermon on that mount of hay, I'll never forget the sweet crooning of the four of us together. Tom sang lead, John sang tenor, Jill sang alto, and I covered the bass. O, if we'd only had a recorder I'm sure we could have sold millions of copies of our holy, sanctified, prophetic and challenging worship music!

It was one song in particular that made my morning. The glory of God was so tangible as to be touchable as we warbled through "I'll Fly Away." It was, I believe, heavenly in harmony and truth: "Just a few more weary days and then, I'll fly away!" At least it was for me, for I've never forgotten, and in spite of the sore muscles, won't forget to include that cowboy conjured reflection when I make my glory report at Home.

"I'll Fly Away"

PSALM 55:5-8

The Psalmist was complaining about the treachery of a friend, a treachery he felt could lead to his death. Before confessing that God's care was sufficient unto his need, he also wished that he had wings like a dove! With them he could fly away and find rest, shelter from the noise and wind/words of his oppressor.

But would flying away help? Running from God doesn't make sense when we've got our senses about us and recognize that only in God's company can we know divine sufficiency as our own.

REFLECTION

The gift of this Psalm for me is in the realization by its author that the only place of true refuge, the only shelter from the fear of harm and death, could be found in flight into the arms and care of the God to whom he prayed. There the enemy would be conquered or subdued, and the dove would be secure.

The evidence of grace in the prayer is that in the end, whether challenged and afraid or sheltered and secure, the only one worthy of trust is the loving God of grace!

When was the last time you needed such refuge? Where did you fly to find it?

Has your trust in God ever found you wanting?

If nothing else, how gracious is the promise of God that when we fly away from this life we fly into eternal joy at Home!

I'll Fly Away

"Honeysuckle Sweet"

Matthew 14:22-33
"Where's your faith? I say, 'come' and you say, 'me?'"

I was back in the panhandle, returning to work on the ranch after a short vacation. A glorious spring morning's cool caught me by surprise and put a new step of joy in my walk to the barn. The task at hand was simple: rake and shovel up the manure that had accumulated over the winter in the front lot and hauls it to the dump. I knew what I was in for in both sight and smell. But I was ready for the task, and equipped with a light heart.

Maybe that light-hearted sensitivity made what happened next so significant. I stepped around the back side of the barn to gather my tools and I stopped dead in my tracks. Standing on a season's accumulation of mess: there – what is that? My nostrils flared like Wind rider's as I searched the memory banks, looking through the odor dictionary for help. I needed to identify that smell.

As I searched, I was suddenly transported to the gate out into the alley in town, the place where I was raised. There, growing healthy and green and covered with tiny flowers and bugs buzzing around everywhere: that's honeysuckle sweet I smell!

Sure enough, across the fence from me, growing healthy and green and covered with tiny flowers and bugs buzzing around everywhere: a honeysuckle vine. The odor dictionary was closed; the source was identified, and as I gathered my rake and shovel the tears began rolling down my cheeks.

It happens now most every time when I'm blanketed by a cloud of honeysuckle sweet: I remember every detail, every emotion, every sadness, every shock and joy at my mother's instant death to a heart attack, and my dad's slow, agonizing death at the hands of cancer. I no longer sob, and didn't much then because of my faith.

For while I hadn't yet been enabled to put words to my hope, or to verbalize my proposal that, if true, now placed both Mom and Dad with the angels and describing the glory of God found in their human journeys, somehow I knew. So their departure for home was never deeply distressing to me. Yes, I continue to miss their companionship along my own way toward Home. But I now leak tears of thanksgiving.

They weren't cowboys or cowgirls, my parents. I believe they enjoyed who I had become as a man, but their childhood riding time had been limited so they couldn't share my own enthusiasm for this way of life. They easily appreciated my connection to horses and cattle and the land and the labor. But that's not who they were.

They were, though, no less a witness to the possibilities I grew into in my own faith, and could well be the two most responsible for my construction of the proposal that we are, in this human journey away from home, gifted in ways angels don't get to know.

Mom and Dad were two with whom I was privileged to travel for a while. They were living examples of gentleness and service. At times, in their struggles, as with each of us, they were examples of poor God-connections; but mostly they were examples of good God-connections. I'll admit that I benefited most watching and learning from them as they demonstrated good connections of love.

I carried the trash from the house to the alley the afternoon following Mom's death. She was 52. That seemed far too young to me. I carried the trash from the house to the alley the afternoon following Dad's death. He was days short of 75. That seemed far too young to me as well.

And as I rounded the corner of the barn, caught up in trying to identify the scent that drew me up to a stop, I was there again, at the gate into the alley at Mom and Dad's house, being graced by that same sweetness, that same fond reflection: they were living examples of good God-connections.

Their devotions and love, in spite of their imperfections, was a healthy and happy classroom for me. It enables me now to celebrate the pianist and the band director: perhaps a heavenly duet in my symphony? The thought is honeysuckle sweet!

"Honeysuckle Sweet"
MATTHEW 14:22-33

Sometimes we are tossed to and fro by the challenges of life, and it can be frightening. In the loss of parents, for example, the whole of life is scrambled into a new way of life. It can indeed seem as though we are afloat in a boat upon troubled waters with no rescue in sight.

Then, coming to us as if without effort or care, the Messiah offers divine assurance. So we step out to meet him, even upon the tempest, and walk with him in gratitude, until we recognize where we are and begin to sink.

We cry out, "Save me!" And the deepest blessing of the night is that he does, without hesitation or reservation, reaching out to take us by the hand, and perhaps chuckling while chiding, "Why do you doubt me?"

There is honeysuckle sweet in the Savior's soothing presence.

REFLECTION

Honeysuckle sweet always, always brings me back to that alley gate, and remembrances of my parents. Often, they were the agents of grace who held out hands of assurance to me. It's a gift to remember them in honeysuckle sweet.

Who do you reach out to in this life when you think you're sinking into the troubles that are so persistent, or powerful?

Do your experiences with the Living Lord Jesus bring sweet reflection to your mind and heart?

How do you respond to the sweet Savior who reaches out to you, without hesitation or reservation?

"A Dark Empty Space"

John 20:1-18

"Why the tears? Emptiness precedes the Rising!"

Springtime holds its own beauties, like every season of the year, but part of the beauty for me has always been watching the baby calves get their legs under them, learn to feed, try and keep up, and discover how to dance together.

It's just a time of new birth all the way around, with the calves and the flowers and the trees and grasses all waking from their winter snooze. And while, yes, the wind can howl across the plains perhaps as a part of the birthing pain of nature, it's a deeply pleasant time of the year.

It's also a time when we moved cattle from pasture to pasture, rotating herds in and out, giving the land time to rest and recoup its vitality, and in that replenished growth to feed hay-weary cows the sweetness of protein rich buffalo grass, and the dessert delights of yucca blooms.

When one of those early spring moves drew close, I had the task of riding the middle pasture on the LZ spread, checking the fences so that the cows and babies we moved in there would stay in there. I loaded a small saddle bag with staples, pliers, wire and such, strapped a wire stretcher to my saddle, and headed out.

This was one of my favorite jobs because it took me into a solitary haven where the sounds of the wind in the creek-bottom trees, the songs of the birds, and the smells of the morning cool were invigorating.

But this particular day held a surprise for me and Popeye. I later penned this response:

I don't remember how many times
I'd been in that middle pasture before,
scouting for cows and babies and
delighting in the nature of the day's chores.

But I'll never forget the coyote den that day
when I was surprised by a couple of howls,
pups at the doorway to a dark empty space,
a small cave I'd never seen before now.

They were memorable to say the least,
but what caught me up with surprise
was how their secret place reminded me
this was Easter time, the week before Sonrise!

It's all about such an empty space isn't it?
It's about a sacrifice of mercy and love
that transforms the death stench of a dark tomb
into the sweet gift of eternal hope from above!

Thank you, Lord, for blessing a simple cowboy
out doing the simple work of a springtime day,
with the renewal of a Sonrise remembrance
and a hope that comes in no other way!

"A Dark Empty Space"
JOHN 20:1-18

They went and found the tomb of the Master empty. They were beside themselves wondering what had happened. The disciples went back home, but Mary stood outside the tomb weeping.

Angels asked her why she was crying: "Someone has taken my Master and I don't know where he is!"

Then a man she thought to be the gardener asked her why she was crying, who she was looking for, and he spoke, saying only, "Mary."

And in the call of her name she recognized him. It was her Master, not stolen or dead, but very much alive!

REFLECTION

As sojourners in a strange and foreign land far from Home, it's so very easy to get locked up in the dirty details of the here and now that we forget the Story!

When was the last time you were surprised to be reminded of the glory of that dark empty space, even in the midst of the ho-hum or the challenge of life!

We forget that we are invited to remember Easter every moment of our lives here, even to remember that Easter's victory is part of our assurance of a Home to return to. How do you remind yourself, trick your brain into making connection with that promise even in the midst of this strange journey?

What emotions and thoughts flood your being when you stop and really remember the significance of that dark empty space?

A Dark Empty Space

16

"Walking the Bubble Around"

Jeremiah 31:2-3; 2 Corinthians 12:8-9
"No matter where you are, I'm there, with sufficient grace."

One of my favorite parts of a year is that time when we move steers and heifers off of the leased wheat pasture up on the flats down to the grass along Wolf Creek on the ranch.

I have nothing against the flats. In fact I love the flats, for those deep moonless nights when you can look from horizon to horizon without trees or homes or hills breaking up the view and can actually see the lights of small towns glowing up to 30 miles away, right at that place where earth meets sky. Or in any given day you can peer into the deepest blue overhead and see all the way to the next galaxy! Or you can watch clouds form and disappear, or build and mass together a thunderstorm coming at you from two states away.

But I also knew the challenges of working the flats in winter, when water had to be hauled to those wheat pastures, and how often that particular job put a body in the elements, in the midst of freezing winds and rains, upon frozen ground, or fighting the snow-melt mud that could suck a boot or a pickup in like "I'm not letting go" tar!

I enjoyed those springtime days on the flats when we carried portable panels and horses in trailers so we could gather those pasture herds, load them out, and transport them to the ranch. Usually the work was manageable if not smooth, and well worth it when the cattle were turned out on the grass.

However, as in all ranch work, it seems there is always a prospect for disruption, of the best laid plans coming apart at the seams, or at the tailgate.

That's what happened one spring morning when after gathering about a hundred steers, and moving four trailer loads successfully, we assumed our work was about complete when we headed south with the final loads.

The morning's dense wet fog had not slowed us a bit. We simply worked carefully and thoroughly, every animal was accounted for, and the moving was about done. Then it happened. As Lawrence made his turn off the state highway the bumping of the road home apparently worked the latch on his trailer loose, for a cowboy never, ever, leaves a trailer gate without double and triple checking to make sure it's latched securely.

So the bump of the new road had to have knocked that latch loose, the gate swung open about a foot, and suddenly, watching from the pickup coming up behind, I stared at a steer as it dropped out of the trailer onto the road, then a second, a third, and more!

Acting with cowboy quickness and cunning, I reached for the CD, I mean the old CB radio and hollered for Lawrence to stop! Luckily, Tom and I got to that gate before the whole load was dumped, and since the turn had been made slowly the cattle were unharmed.

The question was, how do we handle our impromptu creation of a small bunch of dazed steers! It was decided that Tom and Lawrence would continue on to the ranch, then return with horses and portable fencing so we could gather and reload this dumped bunch.

That was fine, except it meant I was elected, appointed, and/or otherwise told to keep an eye on this impromptu herd, to keep them together, and to keep them close enough to the road that we could be seen when horses and fence arrived.

So I dutifully surrendered and gladly and slowly walked into the field they had gathered in and just hung out there until they started migrating away from me. I continued to walk softly so as not to spook them, and they moved with increasingly unforced confidence down the direction of the road.

As we gently progressed along our way I became aware of an incredible phenomenon. I noticed that it was as if we were moving in harmony together under a giant fog bubble, a dome of clearer air we could see each other through, but beyond which lay unknown terrain, terrors or treasures.

And everywhere we went, that bubble went. I almost felt like a pea under a shell that a magician was sliding along at his pleasure, trying to hide us from a dupe who had put money on whether we could be found or not. It was a bit unnerving and a lot awesome, which reminded me how fragile life really can be.

Then the mystery of it all birthed meditation. The bubble became a haven of privacy and sensitivity before the Lord. The magician became divine, and the moments became holy. For in the midst of the mist and the tranquil quiet there was bestowed an assurance that this unique bubble of space was likely never to be known again. It was a blessing for this day alone. And there, as we walked our bubble around together and yet alone, I discovered the intangible touch of God was no less valid or certain than the palpable wetness of the fog.

Under that dome of disruption, following an unplanned order of hours, I was gifted with a flush of profound gratitude that no matter where I was, there God was also, to comfort, direct, and encourage, even and perhaps specifically in the fog of this cowboy morning of surprise and sweet surrender.

"Walking the Bubble Around"
JEREMIAH 31:2-3
While the people of God were in exile, they may well have felt lost, isolated, far from being found, perhaps never to return home. However, the Prophet spoke God's promise that even as far away as they were, divine grace and faithfulness were offered by God to the people, even there!

2 CORINTHIANS 12:8-9
No matter how weak we may feel, or what need we may think we have, God has promised that divine grace is sufficient to our every need. In our weakness, then, we can cry out all the more with gladness as the power of Christ dwells within and through our weakness!

It's just incredible to find that in such weakness, the grace of God is all the more powerful and significant and redemptive and transforming than in moments of strength.
Praise be to God!

REFLECTION

It was really weird at first, being so totally isolated from anything more than that small patch or ground I shared with that handful of disoriented cattle. It was as if I'd been dumped off in the middle of who knew where, and the feeling was one of almost total helplessness.

Then the Spirit of God enabled me to see from high above, from His perspective, and it was only a bubble, that moved around me as I walked, and I knew I was secure in the sufficiency of God's care, no matter how far from the familiar I may have been!

Recognizing what appears to be trouble as potential moments for rejoicing is not always easy. How have you dealt with past troubles and been surprised to find God there, in the midst of it all?

When has God transformed your weakness into the strength of holiness?

"A Tuba, A Camera & A Stampede"

Romans 12
"So give your whole life, all of it, to the Lord who teaches and equips you to love like Christ."

It's fascinating how surprising rodeos can burst into any given cowboy job and wreck havoc on the day. But it's also a deep pleasure to be an integral part of a well-oiled machine in the unfettered accomplishment of labors before us, especially as infrequently as that seems to take place.

While I can remember many a spring branding when a crazy bull has taken out a fence, or a wild cow has taken off for who knows where with her baby, or a damp morning slows the fire building and iron heating, or a rattlesnake under the wood pile scatters cowboys and tools every which way in the surprise, I can also remember when things went like clockwork.

Those were the rare times when plans were clear, the weather cooperative, the roundup faultless and fun, and every cowboy knew his place and his job. Such was the case one spring on the M-Cross ranch. A crew had gathered for multi-tasking, working everything from preg-testing to vaccinating, ear tagging to branding.

The cowboys present were skilled at many of those tasks, but each was assigned a specific job and things worked quite smoothly as we ran everything through the chute. I was chosen to run the catch bar, to catch the head of each animal as it came into the chute believing it had a clear shot at freedom out the end.

As it turned out, once an animal was caught I was also hands-free to help lower one of the squeeze bars so a hot branding iron could be applied. At the same time a cowboy was also vaccinating and another was preg-testing. Others were running the lanes and separating cattle, marking cattle as pregnant or for sale or to be moved back onto pasture and such.

Afterward, some of the separated bunches were loaded, some were pushed into the pasture and herded back west, and some were pinned for later release in the home pasture.

As I look back on that highly successful and mostly pain free day, I am grateful for the camaraderie of the collected crew, the things we shared in common and cared about together, and marvel at how cleanly the job was done.

Sure, part of my strongest sense of joy in being a cowboy is found in the lone hours of building fence. For me, there's nothing much better in life than being way out there in the pasture alone, carrying wire and staples and pliers and tying up broken fences, nailing loose wires up tight, and dreaming and scheming and praying and watching a day unfold and fold back again.

In those moments when the focus is sharply directed in my own little world, it's easier to find solitary wildflowers at my feet, or to watch a mama antelope with her unique twin babies cautiously peer at me as I walk away, then dash for the fence on their way to a safer location. What a thrill to watch her leap the five-wire fence as if it was no higher than a toadstool, and to watch her twins slide under the bottom wire with the ease of a breeze under a horse's belly!

But on this particular day it was the company of those cowboys, the feasting at the lunchtime spread together, and finishing the day with simple satisfaction that captured my imagination.

It dawned on me like the shear pleasure of a multi-colored sunrise that we were each a part of something special that day. We each had a job, we each performed to our capabilities, we enjoyed and respected the talents and the company of one another, and we felt useful and fulfilled at the day's end.

For some reason my mind wandered beyond it all though, to a place where I recognized how God has blessed me with many different talents and pleasures. So I wondered how or why it was that I should find myself at the end of a chute through this kind of an amazing day.

It could have been just as easy for me to end a day of using my art skills with paints or pencils in hand, or to end having sung a "Gloria" or a hymn using my vocal gifts. It might even have been possible to end a day at rehearsal with a symphony as I played
the tuba I enjoy so much. Or I could have ended by writing a radio or print story or shooting photos as a reporter, or by grading papers that I had assigned as a teacher.

I suppose it could also have ended with my tending a night herd while playing the tuba on horseback, and then taking pictures of the stampede that bombastic serenade would surely start! But this day ended on a ranch as a contented cowboy.

The glory of the day was seen in the ways we worked together, each at our own given tasks, skill and pleasure a vital part of the whole, and with each held in high regard, grace and thanksgiving.

Rodeos can be divine if viewed through faith-lenses, and so can a day void of tubas, cameras, and stampedes!

"A Tuba, a Camera, and a Stampede"
ROMANS 12

"Take your everyday, ordinary life – your sleeping, eating, going-to-work and walking-around life – and place it before God as an offering.

"Each of us finds our meaning and function as a part of Christ's body.

"Love from the center of who you are; don't fake it."

What if I don't know what the center of me looks like? Hmmm. Maybe I can find it by keeping company with the Savior, by learning from the Messiah!

REFLECTION

Perhaps the one thing that blesses me most when I consider the life, death, and resurrection of Jesus is that no matter what came his way, he lived his life in total honesty and amazing grace. Nothing, NOTHING kept him from being who God made him to be, or doing what he came to do. And in all things he loved from the very center of who he was and is as Lord and Savior of the world!

I suppose I could have emulated Roy Rogers throughout my life. But there came a point when I was invited to take the Master as my example, and to invite the Holy Spirit to grow my up more like him, as the uniquely gifted and blessed child of God I am, and to live with steadfast trust and faithfulness as far as possible in this life.

Too often I fall away from that ideal. And time and again the Master accepts me back into the fold of divine forgiveness and guidance. And every time, I find lessons that inform and shape my tomorrows.

I'll never ever forget that closely perfect day of cowboying. As easy is it is to remember disasters and unexpected rodeos, so it ought to be that easy to remember the days without such surprises.

What life surprise or rodeo do you most readily remember just now? What happened that made it so memorable? How does that experience inform your life today?

Do you remember a day without such surprises? As thankful as we are invited to be for God's presence in the midst of surprise rodeos, when were you last equally thankful for a day of calm?

As you love from the very core of your being, from the Spirit within you, do you grow to find that even the unexpected is less surprising than when you live in chaos directed by selfishness or fear or judgment?

Where does a day of peace come from? How can we know those days more frequently?

A Tuba, A Camera & A Stampede

"Cowboys 'n Indians"

Matthew 16:24; 2 Peter 1:3-11
"Look – I give you everything you need to come, follow me."

W e were so supremely self-sufficient when we were kids, weren't we, all of us? Maybe that sufficiency has changed in my own kids, but for those of us touched in front and back by Baby Boomers, we just thought we had the world by the tail and we'd never have to let go.

After all, Hoppalong Cassidy and Roy Rogers and Bat Masterson and Sky King and Flicka and Rowdy and Matt and Tonto and the Lone Ranger and big John Wayne and so many others were the living truth, right?

Well, they were in my world of growing up with long sticks that made perfect rifles and short sticks that fit my small palm like a six-shooter. Then there were the limbs and sticks that made bows and arrows and knives. I don't remember ever shooting a homemade arrow over ten feet – not too dangerous! But when we grew into bb-guns, our folks laid down the law of the west: don't shoot at each other! We were thrown in jail more than once for breaking that one.

I used to wonder why it was that I always wanted to be an Indian when we kids played along the creek or in the back yard, but grew up to be a cowboy! Why would I want to be one of those deadly Red-skins who were always subdued or run off or killed in living black and white?

Then my mom told me that there was Indian blood in my family, that my paternal grandmother's great-grandmother was full-blooded Choctaw, and that my maternal great-grandmother grew up with a best friend named Little Red Feather. I suppose it was those earliest stories that birthed a natural affinity in me for the Indians we pretended to be, or to kill.

But I must admit that I was blessed to grow into a cowboy, not as one who seemed always to be in a fight with the Indians, but as a boy who worked with cows from the security of a deep saddle! I tried bareback riding several times when I was younger and had a devil of a time staying aboard. Then many years later, a friend and I helped our friend Bobby catch up a couple of his horses out of an M-Cross pasture, and I volunteered to ride Snips bareback to the corral where our saddles were while they took the pickup in search of the other horse we were after.

Either that was the boniest horse I've ever sat astride, or my fanny is slender enough not to provide the padding I needed for making that a comfortable experience!

Aside from that little raw boned detail, implanted by television's images of Indians riding their beautiful paint ponies with only a blanket serving as saddle, I was drawn to our Native American brothers and sisters by a deeper sense of kinship.

The kinship of which I speak is that of Jesus, the One

come as Savior and Redeemer, the Way-shower home to Heaven. Before I grew into a young man of reason, to a place where I could consider for myself such things as salvation and eternity, I asked my mom thousands of questions about God and faith. She once told me I asked more questions of substance and importance by the age of five than she thought I'd ask in my entire childhood.

So I was gifted with what seems to have been an inborn inquisitiveness about such things, and I asked her, "Why are the cowboys and Indians always fighting?"

I can hear her response as clearly today as I did so many years ago: "They are driven by different dreams."

What a trigger that was for my young imagination and inquiry. Driven by different dreams? Only in later years did I see what she was talking about, and how profound her insight was.

And how incredible such universal truth can be: don't we each live and breathe and labor to make some sort of dream come true? And doesn't that truth frequently set us at odds in this world away from our heavenly home?

But beyond that, is there any way on earth, in this human experience together, to share a cooperative hope even if our dreams are somewhat different? Why can't cowboys and Indians at least live side by side with appreciation if not perfect harmony?

Years later the remembrance of our conversation sparked a poetry response:

Mama, why is that man laughing?
And why is his face painted?
Mama, why is that man almost naked,
and where is he going – like that?

Son, the red man paints his face with laughter
because he needs little clothing to be fully dressed,
and because he's going nowhere,
since he needs go nowhere else to be at home!

Listen to him, my son, that you might be so free.

Truth is, not all dreams are compatible. They can be so different, in fact, that the conflict can cause considerable upheaval, and verbal, spiritual, and physical warfare.

Mom asked me in her own special way, what's your dream?

In this culture's lingo that question has become, "Who's your daddy?" In other words, who or what dream do you serve, do you labor to please or acquire, and what's your motive?

I thank God for God! I am so deeply grateful for the divine option that Jesus offers: "If you want to come home with me, you've got to let me lead the way!" Then he equips us with everything we need for the journey.

Bullets zing through the air and arrows fly, both with deadly possibilities. And there, in the midst of the mayhem and madness is Jesus inviting one and all to a different way, to the way that leads home.

I live in awe of my Abba, Papa, Father, the One who wants me home as badly as I want to be there. There's symphony construction underway here, with cowboys and Indians playing flutes and tubas side by side!

"Cowboys 'n Indians"

MATTHEW 16:24

If we plan to go Home with Jesus, we've got to let Jesus work from the driver's seat, not us! That means giving up the side-seat and back-seat drivers' licenses we claim are from God, but in truth know they're really from fear.

2 PETER 1:3-11

Don't put it off, don't hesitate: accept God's invitation to follow Jesus Home! As you do, you will experience a maturing in faith and faithfulness in discovering your old sin way of life has been wiped from the books, and your new life of grace is taking on the character of Christ himself. The character of CHRIST himself?!?! Really? Yes!

REFLECTION

So many things in this life separate us because we think we're in charge, and our personal agendas become our god. And as often as we lean into that human leadership, we separate ourselves from God and from one another. It's no wonder there is so much strife, trouble, and disappointment between us – we are dreaming different and selfish dreams!

When we accept Jesus' proposal that he drive/lead us home his way, we discover a totally new way of living, and grow in the truth that we were created to live side by side, supporting one another along the same way to the same Home.

How long after you found yourself wandering in the wilderness most recently did it take you to remember God's offer of guidance? Did you receive the invitation out with ease and gratitude, or did you fight that too?

Have you ever been united with someone you once felt

to be an enemy, to live in harmony rather than at war? How surprised were you at God's grace in that relationship? Do you know that such grace comes only as a gift from God?

Why do we struggle so mightily to protect what's not getting us Home, and strive so successfully to remain in the driver's seat when we know we can't make progress until we take the passenger seat?

19

"The Christmas Blizzard"

Luke 2:15-20
"Holler! Shout! Introduce the world to the Prince of Peace!"

In my books there's just no right or good time for a blizzard to dump itself on you. The complications from having too much snow packed too high for too long are without number.

Under those conditions it can be easy to lose your grip on the incredible and powerful good sense, wisdom, and humor so much a part of being who a cowboy is in heart and courage.

And I suppose I shouldn't offer excuses or apologies when that happens because it just agitates and aggravates when I wake in the morning to find three to four-foot drifts of snow everywhere, cold whistling through naked tree branches, and horses and cattle scattered to the four winds over snow-covered fences.

One of the most significant moments in my life fell upon me like one of those heavy blizzards one December. It fell with such force that even 4-wheeler travel was next to impossible, so most of what needed to be done had to be done horseback. But the horses had to be found and brought home first!

Once that was done, our work was slow, cold, and quiet. I guess it will never cease to amaze me how quiet it gets after a good snow blankets the ground. No more crunching of dry grass or hooves kicking stones by man or beast. No more road noises as trucks roll down pasture tire ruts. Even what birds are around seem to hunker down for a spell to catch their bearings, to gather themselves after the snow-dance that transforms the landscape into a white-washed wonderland.

The surreal sense of such a day caught me up short not too long after this particular blizzard. Our work had been completed for the day, and as I walked back to the house from the saddle shed, I was surprised by that silence and stopped cold in my tracks. Still and amazed, I let my senses take charge as my skin shivered, my nose picked up the fresh crispness of the air, my ears blew open in search of missing typical ranch noises, my heart beat so steadily that its rhythm was all I could hear, and my eyes were shocked by the magical sights of both the first evening stars and a light snowfall that had begun.

As I stood there and soaked it all up I began to wonder, could it have been a night like this when those innocent and simple shepherds were blown out of their comfort zones by an angel – the one who came announcing the arrival of the Messiah?

And what went through their minds and hearts as that angel chorus joined in singing "Hallelujah!" to the newborn King of Kings?

Say what? Find me a rock to hide under! Help, Lord, Help!!!

Then I was spooked, perhaps frightened as those shepherds were by an unexpected sound. For me, it was a branch that cracked and fell to the ground. Enough snow had finally collected there to bring it down with a snap, pop, and crash!

Instantly I was transported to the place where I heard the story about the dove and the wise old owl. It seems that the two of them were perched on a tree branch together when it began to snow.

The owl asked the dove, "How much does a snowflake weigh?"

"Nothing more than nothing," was the answer.

The owl then told the dove about another snow, the time he was sitting on a branch and as he had nothing better to do, he decided to count the snowflakes that fell on that particular branch. He counted upward to 37,451,787 snowflakes, and then when the 37,451,788[th] flake landed on his branch, weighing nothing less than nothing, the branch broke and fell to the ground.

With that the surprised dove flew away. And the wise old owl, who seemed an expert on the matter, reflected, "Perhaps there is but one more voice to be heard for peace to come to the world."

The shepherds made their way to the manger, so they could see for themselves God's gift of the Prince of Peace to this world. Then they went home and let loose in praising and worshipping the glory of the Lord!

My voice was much quieter, but when I returned to the house, I couldn't keep quiet. I had to relay my remembrance to the family, and wonder with them, "Whose voice is it that's needed for peace to come to the world? Is it mine?"

Amazing, what a nasty blizzard can conjure up in the life of simple shepherds, and simple cowboys!

"The Christmas Blizzard"
LUKE 2:15-20

The angel choir was gone, and the shepherds were left there alone to decide what they would do next. They decided to go into town to see what the heck the angels had been singing about! So they went, quickly, and found it just as they had been told. They also told everyone what had happened, and how their night watch had been interrupted with a divine proclamation.

Then, while Mary kept their words in her heart, the shepherds returned to their work, rejoicing in the Lord, with new-found trust in finding that everything was just as they had been told!

REFLECTION

Sometimes it seems so easy to believe the national and/or local media, and the beauty shop and/or co-op gossip, and so incredibly hard to believe what the Word tells us, or the Holy Spirit whispers in our hearts. Why is it so easy to believe the information our fallen world floods our lives with, and so tough to believe what God offers in love?

Sometimes we don't even test what the world offers as truth, and can't believe anything we receive from the Lord without a thorough discussion/test. How do we get to the place where we test the world, and trust the Lord?

Is there a "voice of peace" in your life? Are you a voice for peace in the lives of your circle of influence?

Is the Prince of Peace your Prince of Peace?

"Giving in and giving up . . ."

Galatians 1:1-5
"The promise is grace, forever, and I won't quit believing."

As I look back, now many, many years beyond my growing-up days in the wide open spaces of the Texas panhandle, I reflect with true gratitude. I was privileged to live in the company of a loving, nurturing, and supportive family with friends of the same ilk, and to taste what I felt certain was the sweetness of genuine peace.

There, along the banks and among the towering cottonwood trees of Wolf Creek, I learned to sit quietly enough to watch a raccoon grab minnows for supper, to witness the birth of baby calves, and to peer so deeply into the star-spangled night that I felt I might have caught a glimpse of the very gates of Heaven.

Only in growing up and being invited to live out the rest of my life as a *responsible* adult in this world did I begrudgingly step beyond the freedoms of my childlike perceptions of truth to a place where they grew dim, like long-ago and flickering dreams.

It wasn't until I could read the papers myself, and watch the black and white television videos of President Kennedy's assassination, that I began to understand this human experience is dangerous. Living, I discovered, can get you killed!

Then came Viet Nam's war that we were told wasn't a war but that killed beloved American soldiers just as lifeless as any war before or since. The protests were as vivid in my heart as they were on college campuses and county courthouse lawns, and I personally had to ask myself if I would go, or retreat to someplace like Canada if I were drafted. It ended before I had to execute my choice.

Before I graduated from college I had joined the world in giving in and giving up on those childhood dreams about tranquility and peace and kindness ruling us together. As my world and awareness expanded, my comfort and joy wilted into tiny remnants of hope. With the evils of war and inflation, global warming and rampant disease, and so much more, it became easy for me to be glad I had learned to use a gun, safely, long ago in Junior NRA. And I was gladdened by the thought that I'd taken the time to teach my boys how to do the same, for surely the time would or will come when, as with our forefathers in this beloved nation, we must depend on them for hunting and survival.

Such is the remembrance and imagination of a boy grown to a man. But I thank God Almighty for the work of those who have gone long before us, those who worked with fearless faith to teach us that as evil as this world is when we individuals and societies live in separation from God, so all the more abundant is the freedom and hope purchased for us in the grace and peace of God evident in a tomb emptied by divine love rather than worm and centuries. My conviction is simple: this is not all there is to it.

Yes, it seems quite evident and obvious that what Lao-Tzu once wrote is true, that weapons are instruments of misfortune, and that those who are violent do not die naturally. But I would not complete the thought there, by giving in and giving up to the power of such human limitations and inventions.

Paul, in writing to the church in Galatia, bears my soul up to a different place, to a place high in the Texas panhandle if no other, where in remembering the simplicities of childhood recollections I find myself supremely grateful for his experience-born assurance that the power of God is yet supreme and victorious, and in living life from God as a gift we can indeed live life that is whole.

The other side of human fear and desolation is the grace and peace of divine promise and hope. While it is not easy, and must be done moment by moment, in this particular moment I choose not to give in or give up that promise and hope to fear and desolation. At God's invitation, I choose the fearlessness of hope's grace and peace!

How delightful it is today that when I ride across those same Wolf Creek nooks and crannies of my childhood I am transported back to those days! Vividly I see the same sights and hear the same sounds and smell the same smells and feel the same breezes and watch the same miracles. It's almost as though I don't have to write a symphony of glory and praise because God has written it for me!

Do I dare plagiarism? Naw! My offering is divinely ordained and will be sweet music in its own unique way.

"Giving in and giving up . . ."
GALATIANS 1:1-5

Paul knew himself to be God-commissioned in his work as a missionary/witness to the word of the Risen Christ. He worked with diligence and courage because he knew that there was so much more to *life* than what lay before our eyes!

Paul knew from personal experience that the resurrected Jesus had made a sacrifice that cleansed all who would believe in Him, and knew through his own rescue that what Christ offered to him, Christ offered to all: the rescue of grace and peace!

REFLECTION

At times the troubles of this fallen world can drag even experienced cowboys down into depression or dismay, robbing them of the joy of such unique work among God's wide open spaces. For those who stick with it, sometimes through a tough day, and at other times through extended drought or down markets, they discover that they didn't have to give in or give up in the face of challenges. When did you last face a tough challenge to your way of life, or your daily comfort, and in dismay consider giving in or giving up and letting that challenge rule?

When, in the midst of a challenge, were you shocked, or pleased, or even amazed at a God-thang that rescued you from the doldrums and offered to you the divine peace of God's own grace?

Have you ever given in or given up the struggle, and later had to start over? Can you sense the value of even that experience as it informs your choices when next you are challenged?

"The Piggin-strang"

James 1:16-21; Psalm 145:3
"We learn compassion and mercy from the Master alone."

It's true that most of the time a real cowboy works from sunup to sundown and beyond. The hours can be long and the work grueling day after day. However, there are times when Mother Nature can bring things to a halt with rain storms or blinding snows.

I remember well the winter that was so cold we didn't much go outside except for insuring survival of the livestock. We'd feed and doctor as needed, and then spend time in the warmth of the house. It was that particular winter Tom taught me how to work with leather, and I made a couple of belts I can still wear today – cowboy foresight prompted me to make them a bit longer than I needed at the time!

And while I still use one of those belts for work, and the other as a dress belt, the thing I remember most vividly about my leather work still hangs on a gate post in the north pasture as a reminder that observing boundaries in this life is mostly a choice.

Sometimes the boundaries around us are easy to observe because consequences for flaunting, stretching, or "busting loose" from them can bring swift response. It doesn't take too many speeding tickets to make the point clear: the highways are not a place for racing the clock, or another cocky cowboy.

Other boundaries are less convincing. I mean, we're told that using tobacco in any of its varied forms can kill. But try convincing a cowboy who's chawed a hunk for 30 or 40 years of the threat, the boundary, and you're liable to catch a spitewy on the toe of your boot! It may not be until the gum and teeth rot and cancer is confirmed that such a boundary is considered viable.

Frequently we don't like boundaries any more than a 2000 pound bull likes a fence or a gate, so like that bull we just jump or bust 'em.

It's wondrous to me, though, that in busting boundaries we often find ourselves bound to an isolation or a protection we had grown to take for granted, instead of free to act any way we see fit and expect consequences afforded by those old limitations.

That stubborn insistence on having our own way, often at any price, can cost us more than we know until it's too late. Bust through a fence, take off for the hills, find yourself without the comforts of feed or cowboy-vet services, then make your way back to a repaired and improved fence and find yourself locked out! In the weakened position caused by such stubbornness, is there strength enough to jump or bust your way back into the safety of those important boundaries?

I was offered a lesson in humility the spring after a particularly hard winter, after I'd braided myself a fancy new piggin-strang from a blend of black and brown leather strips. It was long and limber, six strings woven together in such a way I thought they were unbreakable. I was one proud winter weary cowboy!

The shock of that spring afternoon was captured this way:

I used to think I was a seasoned cowboy
capable of handling most any job required
as I went about the business on the place
where I'd always dreamed of being hired.

I could ride high with the best of them I thought,
on stallion or mare, bronc or green-broke,
and I could mend fence or brand the babies
as efficient and quick as orders were spoke.

But the day came when my mighty attitude
was offered a lesson in embarrassed humility,
and I'll never forget that busted pasture gate
whose proper closing was my responsibility.

The total ranch Hereford herd upwards of 400
had been gathered together for count and inspection,
and as the last drag through I was to shut the fence
and keep 'em headed in a homeward direction.

But something spooked a mama way up front
and before my agile cowboy response could be made
the whole crazy bunch was turned and headed back
like they were on some wild cow herd run and raid!

Sadly, as quickly and tightly as I'd bound that gate up
with my brand new hand-braided piggin-strang,

they busted through like it weren't even there;
it sounded like a rifle shot with an ear-busting bang!

Mercy, I was so proud of that leather masterpiece
wound with cowboy-expertise and showoff pride.
But at the end of the day and its hard dusty work
that fence gate found a herd on the derned wrong side!

I'm grateful today for that experience, and wonder if part of that piggin-strang may yet hang on the fence up north. But more than that, I'm grateful for the remembrance. It still teaches me today that the greatness of our gracious God is sometimes measured not in freedoms found in faith so much as the divine fences, boundaries designed to keep us safely out of harm's way.

In truth, I find that the road home is often a road far less traveled in part because it's a narrow way, and its limitations are perhaps less appealing in this culture than what appears so harmless on the other side of the fence. But this road is the only way home, and those limitations are designed to protect and encourage us all along the way.

"The Piggin-strang"
JAMES 1:16-21

There is but one way home, so don't get thrown off course by a two-faced fickle world. Trust the trustworthy God, who is a divine gardener who landscapes the faithful to be a salvation-garden forever!

And we're not talking about spinach and turnips here. We're talking about the sweet grace of contentment and joy!

PSALM 145:3

While there are boundaries in the garden God wants to make of us, God does what God promises – there are no boundaries to God's greatness and love!

Can you imagine being the apple of His eye?

REFLECTION

Sometimes the advertisements and temptations of this fallen world are spiced with sweet lies and false hopes. And while we claim to be people of faith, we are yet deeply pulled in those directions, away from the company and love of God.

The struggle seems at times to be endless! And in spite of the fact that the truth of the world's emptiness is revealed at every turn along the roads leading away from God, we yet too often give them a try, walk outside the boundaries or limitations of faith, and find ourselves lost and alone.

Thank God for the open invitation to come back! Thank God that in the Risen Christ every enemy we might face, including death itself, is overcome for us! And thank God for the boundaries/guidelines/limitations that safeguard those who trust God and obey divine will.

So, when were you farthest from home as a person of faith?

When did you find yourself crossing a fence against God's will most recently?

What emotions do you experience when you are discovered, or you realize that you are outside God's boundaries?

How do you deal with being on the wrong path? How do you get back on the path that leads home to God?

What kind of piggin-strangs have you busted, or been

glad to have found that turned you back?

What words of wisdom, gleaned from personal experiences outside those fences, would you offer to your circle of influence?

"Sweets from the Sweet-giver"

Matthew 11:28-30
"What the Lord asks us to bear is made bearable by His own grace."

No doubt about it, and you know it to be true if you've ever been there, doing the work of a cowboy, or a cowgirl, is just plain tough. Muscles get strained to the limit at times, sweat rolls from your brow to your toes at times, the dust and odors of the labor can gag you at times, the weather can turn from delightful to frozen in an hour at times, dogs or rattlesnakes or ornery cows or cranky pickups can drive you nuts at times!

And yet, there are also those times when all those other times can be so far from your memory that nothing can steal the beauty of it all. I recall rainbow times like that, and wild flowers that literally cover a pasture, and brand new baby calves as they stumble and wobble to get up on their legs for the first time. Those are safe and secure sweet memories for me.

There are just times when you know you've been blessed with the sweetness of life by the giver of all sweetness! In those moments, all you can do is lay your spirit back, take a deep breath, and rest in a way contrary to daily ranch-life demands.

I wish today I could remember the recipe for such rest that we used to take advantage of, on rare occasions I'll admit. It was so infrequent that it was like a holiday! Who knows why it didn't happen more often – perhaps that's why even the memory is so sweet.

It would begin with a "duh!" moment. It's been raining or snowing and work has come to a standstill and we wonder: what now? Well, duh! Let's cook up a batch of donut holes!

What a delightful and messy treat that was, to dig out the recipe that always got lost between the sharing of this rare treat, then scrounging around for the ingredients and sometimes making wishful substitutions for those missing, and then stirring them up into a nice workable batter.

All that while, the deep fryer is heating up and just when the two come together in perfect harmony, donut batter and hot oil, a glob of batter is rolled off the end of a spoon and eased into the heat.

Tender care is given to watch with diligence, lest anything dare be lifted to the drying towels before they are perfectly dark browned and crunchy on the outside. When they are cool enough to handle they are delicately rolled in a powdered sugar and cinnamon mixture, and like magic, they disappear from fingers like coins that disappear into vending machines. Like those coins, once fried, sugared and flicked into the mouth, these sweet treats are gonners for sure.

Washed down with sipped cold milk, or hot coffee, the combination of such sweet treats and unhurried moments never fails to calm frayed nerves, to relax furrowed brows, and to over-stuff empty stomachs.

The aftermath is sometimes uncomfortable for a couple of hours. But we're not going anywhere anyhow, so it seldom matters. And it always seems such a small price to pay for the rest and relaxation, the fellowship and the fun.

I doubt this is what Jesus was seeking to teach when He offered to carry our loads for us and to give us rest. However, if we'd been there to offer Him such a sweet way to rest, I'm certain it would have been at least a small part of what He was talking about.

After all, as the giver of all things sweet, surely the sweet treats and restful moments we indulged in would not be a surprise to Him, and perhaps would have been a delight to Him in His own experiences with divine rest! For surely we considered these sweets from the Giver of sweets to have been delivered from Heaven itself.

"Sweets from the Sweet-giver"
MATTHEW 11:28-30

Ah, to know from personal experience the "rest" of the Messiah, to walk and work with Him in perfect trust of God, to be burdened with nothing beyond our capacity, to keep company with Him! Surely this is to learn the unforced rhythms of divine grace!

So why do we so readily muck it up with personal agendas and fears? When we've first walked with Him, isn't that enough evidence of peace to keep us by His side for the rest of a lifetime?

REFLECTION

Donut holes are indeed a sweet treat. But you and I both know that the kind of sweet relief from our weariness in faith's struggle has little to do with dietary choices. No, the sweet relief of the Master is tied up in our choosing to walk His way, to trust God without compromise or apology, to keep company with and learn first hand from the very giver of true sweetness in life.

Such sweetness is called "the unforced rhythms of grace."

How often in this life do you recognize the intimate presence of Christ in your life? In those moments, do you also recognize the sweetness of His desire to be with you?

In a world more prone to disjointed and disrupted clatter and clutter, how often do you let the world have its way without considering or remembering there is an alternative choice that can be made?

How can you remind yourself of your choices, moment by moment, so at least you will realize your direction?

Knowing you have experienced the sweetness of this world, and the sweetness of faith and faithfulness as well, which do you honestly prefer? Why is it that even knowing the differences between the two, we so often continue to choose the worldly chaos rather than the Christ rhythm?

"A Good Name"

Proverbs 22:1
"In God's company, and in God's ways, we are clearly identified."

It's curious to me how it's such a challenge for some among us to remember names. I fall into that category, at times, such as when I'm tired and ready to drift off to a good night's sleep, or when I'm just awake in the morning and looking for my first cup of hot tea or coffee, or when I'm bone tired at noon after a hard morning's labor, or, well, I guess I'm just not too sharp when in comes to remembering names.

That is, unless there's a certain tag or event or emotion that can be tied to the name I'm trying to remember. For example, I'll never forget the name Apple because that was the first horse to buck me off! And it will always be easy to remember the name Deuce because that's the first horse I fell in love with as an adult.

Thankfully, I've never had trouble remembering my wife's name, or my parents' or sisters' or children's names. But it is a troubling challenge for me at times to remember names of new acquaintances, or people I meet only once or twice.

That's where the tag or event or emotion comes in. The first time I drove a tractor I was a carefree 10-year old kid, but I've remembered the name of the man who hired me from the beginning, since we had the same initials: JHK. And I'll never, ever forget Myron, a big, tall farmer who sang in the church choir, and whose voice dropped off the edge of the world when he sang in his deep, deep bass range. I can only dream about singing like that!

Other names also stuck and were well suited, like the name we gave that fluffy white cowardly dog Marshmallow; or the high-spirited pony whose spirit was so hard to read that he was named Joker.

And I continue to make connection with the old CB days, when "handles" were popular. On the ranch, for example, Lawrence was the "Straw Boss," and was so in part because he was the boss, and in part because when it came time for dealing with hay harvest, he was old enough that he didn't have to lift a finger to watch, guide, and boss the whole operation from his pickup!

Tom chose a handle that fit not only his self-perception, but also the truth of his carriage in the saddle. He was and always will be the "High Loper" to me. The image of the handle revives fond memories as I visualize him on Happy, out working cattle.

Personally, I can't remember why I took or got my own handle. It could have had something to do with how I didn't hesitate to jump to it when something needed done. I could also get plenty done in a hurry if needed. However, I've never had the bushy tail that goes with the "Rabbit." But the handle stuck.

Another handle that I've found myself using more and more frequently through the years is, for me, divine. When it dawned on me that we may receive a gift even angels don't get when we are invited to this human experience, I became more intimately aware of the Lord's activities and presence among us.

When I am pleasantly surprised by wildflowers in the pasture, or blessed with an amazing sunrise or sunset that catches me off guard, or renewed in my own faith at the courage of someone's personal account of healing or hope, I don't hesitate to think even if I don't speak, "Another God thang!"

I've even considered what handle others might tag me with, strangers or new friends, cowboys or not. I find myself praying and hoping they might even consider for me, as I hope I might for others, that there walks and works "Another God thang." I can think of no other name I'd rather have!

"A Good Name"
PROVERBS 22:1

What's in a good name, a sterling reputation? More worth and value than any amount of money in the bank! That includes the truth that even if you're a "Somebody" by name and reputation, rather than a Tom or Hank or John, you're still richer than a bank full of gold.

REFLECTION

I'm sure I've been called a lot of different names, nick-names, or dastardly-terms in my life. Mostly, I've deserved each and every one. I've even named and re-named myself through life, changing one name to another as self-awareness, self-perception, and self-hope have risen and/or fallen with the tides of experience.

When I stop, though, and wonder what name God calls me by, I'm brought up short, with a brow-raised wonder. Scruffy? Punk? Author? Cowboy: *real* cowboy? Kid?

What do you hope God calls you?

What experiences or events have defined your character, and perhaps given evidence from which an appropriate name might be drawn?

Thief? Lazy? Skunk? Failure?

I thank God with you that as people of God's own creative genius and purpose and desire, and through the obedience of Jesus, we are given the choice that gives us the name: son/daughter of God!

How amazing that in the realms of faith and faithfulness we are each known to be "another God-thang!"

So, how do we preserve our true identity before the world, or does that matter?

What is your name?

24

"Students Along the Way"

Matthew 23:1-8

"You are none less than students of the Master, the Messiah!"

Along my own personal journey, I've grown very grateful for the many gifts of life, including the gifts of my teachers. My parents were invaluable to me of course, and I can remember each of my teachers in K-5, as well as many others through high school.

But the teachers that have impressed me the most are those outside of my home and the classroom. These teachers were simply workaday folk who labored to provide for their families, to be responsible participants in the community, and to live with integrity and hope through their faith in God.

Most of the time they didn't know they were teaching me anything, just as I've grown to understand I've unknowingly been a teacher for others, which is sometimes discomforting to consider!

After all, who would want to learn anything from some of the mistakes I've made in and through my own learning process? For example, I was once instructed to repair a couple of benches we used for picnics on the LZ place. As young as I was, I was proud as punch to be asked, and pretty pleased with my handiwork when done.

Then came the test, with the boss gingerly lowering his 220-pound frame to see if the benches would hold him up! I'm glad to report that the first bench he tested held him high. However, well, you can only guess at my red-faced mortification when he sat on the second bench and it collapsed! He hooted and hollered with laughter at the sight of my embarrassment!

Yet that experience, like so many more before and since, taught me how much a person can learn from mistakes and about the relief of laughter in the face of them.

A person can also learn much from the different ways others may choose to do the same job. Setting up portable panels for temporary corrals or catch-pens was one such job. Tom had loads more experience than me. He showed me time and again how he wanted pens put up and was even kind enough to explain his reasoning most of the time.

I don't know how much of his effort sunk into my mind, though, for most every time he left me with the responsibility my designs would call him to make changes or adjustments. I never seemed to get it quite right.

Then one wintry morning he got a call that a heifer was out on one of the wheat pastures up on the flats, again. We'd taken horses and pushed her back into the field where she belonged two or three times since that bunch was turned loose up there, so this time Tom decided we'd catch her and bring her to the ranch, holding her there just until the next sale.

So we loaded the portable panels in one trailer, Happy in another, and headed for the flats. When we got there Tom mounted up and headed out to find that unruly young lady and left me with the job of building a catch-pen before he returned.

I worked quickly, knowing full well that Tom's irritation at the heifer would mean a quick find, sure rope and catch, and drag-if-necessary return. I was pretty proud of myself for finishing in a timely fashion, and for the fact that the crazy critter on the end of his rope was relatively easy to pen and load.

After we stacked the panels back into the trailer, and Happy with that heifer, Tom looked at me with an unusually wry smile and said, "I never would have built a pen like that, but it worked!"

That was a big day for me, and maybe for Tom as well. I had accomplished the task satisfactorily, and Tom admitted that while it wasn't a Tom-job, it was workable, and he didn't need to refine or adjust what I'd done.

It was almost as if he learned something from me that day, or learned something about himself through our different ways.

I don't remember where I read it, but I know I've seen it somewhere: "All of us are teaching something all the time, and there are students everywhere."

More important to me, though, is my perception that we are all students in this human journey, and if we choose to watch and listen to the teacher named Jesus, we are going to be blessed with lessons, sometimes moment by moment, about the ever and always present God who wants us home.

In the warm sunshine of that wintry morning, in the friendship Tom and I will always share, in the accomplishment of a specific task together, and in the potentially revolutionary gifts of knowing a "workable" pen, I found abundant evidence of God's grace, of God's devotion to us, and of the divine ways God chooses to reveal that presence.

We are each different in so many ways. We have had different teachers along the pathway of our journey, and we often learn in unique ways. But we are alike in this: as students here, the glory of God's devotion to us each is true, incredible, and worthy of our total gratitude. What an incredible Teacher we sit before!

"Students Along the Way"
MATTHEW 23:1-8

There are plenty of folks who would like for us to believe that they are faultless authorities and that we can and should follow their lead and instruction without fail or complaint. Perhaps the content of their message has viability, but they themselves are not much more than puffed up fashion shows!

Be careful not to let others put you, who believe in the God of Christ and God's divine grace, up on a high horse! Speak only with truth, never exalting anything or anyone other than THE Teacher who makes you classmates together as you learn from the Messiah.

REFLECTION

Think back for a moment: who is the single most influential teacher you have ever studied under, learned from, and hold the highest regard for? What made that teacher so memorable and honorable?

Have you ever been guilty of placing honorable teachers on pedestals or high horses, making them something more than the good teachers they are?

If we are each of us teachers, and there are truly students everywhere, "How' it going, Teach?" Do you know you are on someone's high horse? Does it feel good way up there, sometimes out of reach?

How do you manage to maintain simplicity in your own faith as you seek to learn from the Teacher as a devoted student?

What is the most important lesson you have received from Him? Do you also know you have the opportunity to teach that lesson in your way of life? What empowers you, the teacher?

"A Day's Daze"

2 Thessalonians 3:6-13

"Don't be wary of work for the Lord, for this is right and good."

It's true for each of us I think, that there are times when we get tired, or we're just lazy for a day. Such idleness is not always bad as it can be a time for reflection, prayer, and meditation. Those are quiet times for me when I find the busyness of the world to be out of sight and out of mind, and the rest is helpful.

The opposite can also be true. There can be times when the world whirls in upon us, when there is so much to tend to that we can't seem to shut off the hours or the mind, and life just brings upon us days that seem like a daze. Sometimes it's good daze, and sometimes it's bad daze!

I'll never forget the first invitation I received to cowboy after our call to ministry in the Texas panhandle, following several cowboy-less years in Kansas. It was Bobby calling, inviting me to help with a roundup and branding on John's M-Cross ranch. He called about noon the day before the work and suddenly everything else I had been dealing with or thinking about was shelved in favor of anticipating the next day.

Bobby asked me to meet him at his place around 5:15 the next morning so we could feed, saddle, and load the horses for the 30-40 minute trip south and our planned start time with the sunrise.

Immediately after accepting his invitation and hanging up, my mind went to work on me and I began wondering if, after all these years out of the saddle, I would be up to the full day's work, if I could stay in the saddle if called upon to chase down a less than cooperative calf, or if I would be embarrassed by my rusty ground-skills and dogging babies and vaccinating and ear-tagging, and even before that if I had a pair of jeans for the job, if my old boots needed oiling and loosening up so I wouldn't come home with blister covered feet, and if I needed to wear my straw or felt hat or if I would just wear the one that still fit the best, and the endless list of details just kept flowing at me in a way that at 2 in the morning, with little or no sleep in anticipation of the alarm going off at a quarter of five, I was visualizing myself climbing into an unfamiliar saddle on a new horse that could be a lot more like Popeye than Windrider and I knew I had no choice but to take what was offered, so I wondered if Bobby also had chinks or chaps I could borrow in defense against the Spring morning cool and the brush we might have to negotiate in pursuit of the herd, and if he had a pair of spurs that would fit my boots, and if I'd remembered to buy enough energy bars for us to gobble down just before we began the roundup so we'd not faint from hunger before lunch came around, and how much I was looking forward to another of those seemingly magical moments when a crew of dirty cowboys gathers at the same table to chow down on roast beef and potatoes and carrots and jell-o salads and homemade bread and pie and cake and sweet iced tea and then be so full it was almost painful to get up and get back to the pasture for the second half of the day that would be a daze before it was over! Whew!

Then, with just over an hour before the alarm would sound, after all that had been blowing through my mind and heart, when I had finally worn myself out with the thinking and the questions and the anticipation, I fell into a sleep that seemed to last only a moment before the buzzer rudely roused me back to the morning.

As I rolled up out of sleep, in the dark of that comfortable room and truly inviting bed, it occurred to me that this was the beginning of a new day, a day created by our gracious God, and I was about to embark on a time of joyous, dirty, hard, sweaty, and stinky labor that I loved.

In the midst of the certainty of the day's daze to come I was blessed to find God right there with me, inviting me to receive the gift with glad gratitude and praise. So I did, and the day was a daze, and I was renewed and refreshed in His Company.

"A Day's Daze"
2 THESSALONIANS 3:6-13

The orders are simple: work for your keep. Laziness is not tolerable! And if you do work, don't keep company with those who don't, allowing them to freeload off the workers.

Be diligent in your work/faith then, and don't slack off in any way as you do what the Lord calls you to do. That means even if the post hole you're digging is through a layer of rock, you keep at it, one stone at a time, until you get through to the rich earth beneath that which would stop you in your tracks. One stone, one step at a time.

REFLECTION

When was the last time you had such a busy day that everything seemed to run together? When last did such a day become two, then three days of the same, so that your whole life blew past in a daze of forgettable activity?

So, how did you feel IF you happened to recognize the daze of those days: helpless, hopeful, worn out, blessed?

And how does looking back now make you feel: glad to have survived, sad to have left so much undone, apprehensive about the next day's daze?

What defines the priority of your days, and your labors?

What parameters delineate the measure of success found in those days?

Who do you work for, or should you work for, no matter what your work happens to be?

Does doing your work unto the honor of God make a difference in your attitude and the outcome of those over-busy days? Should it?

IS THIS a day the Lord has made, that you rejoice and are glad in?

"Murphy"

1 Corinthians 4:21
"How shall I greet you: with a fist to the face, or a hug?"

I'll never forget the night I was upstairs trying to sleep in my own bed, but I simply could not because I kept having what were to me nightmares. I don't recall the nature of those distressing dreams, but I do vividly remember creeping my 6-year old fears down the stairs so as not to wake anyone else, tip-toeing into the room beside Mom's bed, rousing her by tugging on the sheet, and asking, "I can't find a sweet dream anywhere upstairs: can I sleep down here with you tonight?"

Her sweet smile is branded in my memory banks, right there beside the warm embrace that welcomed me into her bed, and those arms that wrapped around me with understanding and protection.

I have been deeply and truly blessed in my life, especially in the gift of my parents and who they were, and how they showered me and my sisters with their love. Theirs was a gracious and simple way, with patience beyond my understanding now. As a parent myself I have been faced with challenges that were surely at least the depth of such anguish as I caused them! As I think back on their response to me, I am just in awe of their devotion and kindness. Yes, they were accomplished school teachers; but they were also wise teachers of grace to me.

I remember several occasions when things were distressed in my young life and they were there for me. It didn't matter if it was a dog bite to doctor, a football that needed air, a vocabulary word I needed a definition for, a bike needing repair – in all things I recall, they were there to embrace and teach.

I don't believe that Murphy was as fortunate as I was. Murphy was a dappled gray gelding purchased by Gordon and Jane, who lived part of the time down on the LZ spread, and part of the time in Missouri. Murphy had come out of a feedlot environment and was well trained as a cow pony, and gentle to ride.

Gordon was a retired Naval Master Sergeant who never seemed to me to be in much of a hurry about anything, and carried himself with confidence, but also gentleness. He and Murphy became fast friends quickly, and never gave each other trouble as they worked together.

But something, somewhere in his life, had caused Murphy to live with extreme caution when anyone reached up around his ears or over his head, which made bridling a bit of a chore to accomplish. Murphy was over 16-hands tall, so when he raised his head in self caution as perhaps he remembered a beating once received on the head, it was a long way up there when you tried to put that bridle on!

Now understand here, I'm no expert horse whisperer or trainer, but I've learned a thing or two through the years. One of them is that horses respond to pressure. That's one of the ways cowboys learn to speak horse language. When you push on a horse, the natural response is that the horse will push back. If you want a horse to go left, pressure to the right will invite him to push against you and turn left.

That being true, I tried speaking Murphy's language once when I was given permission to ride him, and it came time to bridle him. Having worked with him before I knew of his head-to-the-sky practice, and understood it was probably the result of an old and painful experience. So on this particular occasion I moved slowly, placing my left hand just above his nose, and inching my right hand with the bridle up his neck until it was just behind his ears.

At that point I applied a gentle pressure downward on both his nose and head, he pushed upward in natural response, and I maintained that gentle pressure until he quit pushing back. Immediately upon his stopping that upward pressure, I stopped my downward pressure. Never removing my hands, after he relaxed I applied the same gentle downward pressure again, and he again pushed up, and I relaxed only when he did.

The third or fourth time I did this, Murphy began to lower his head a bit in response to my pressure. It was as if he had figured out that if he lowered his head instead of pushing up against my pressure, I would quit pushing down. Very quickly after that Murphy's head was down parallel to his back, and the bridle was easily placed and adjusted at my own arm level.

Gordon was impressed, and since I'd never tried this pressure communications before, so was I.

The thing that impressed me most, though, was how painless and fearless and rodeo-less it was and became to communicate with Murphy. Trust was built between us, and it wasn't long before he would lower his head without that pressure when I came to bridle him.

That trust also translated into more confidence and ease together when we worked cattle or simply rode pasture. It was indeed a pleasure to have known and shared the creek with Murphy.

While that experience will surely be a part of my glory and praise report when I'm blessed to return home, so will my report about the gentleness I was blessed with in my parents. I know now how I took that for granted, for I've met many, and counseled some whose experiences with their parents were drastically different from my own.

Many grow through childhood as if it were one long bull ride and bronc busting, and tornado and fence mending after another, with few moments for healing or mercy between them.

Paul invited the Corinthians to choose how he might come to them, as a stern disciplinarian or a gentle teacher. He gave them the choice.

It seems to me that God offers us the same. It grieves me to know that there are those who are not given such a choice and are the sons and daughters of stern and sometimes abusive disciplinarian parents. It grieves me that so many animals are not given such a choice.

But how I do thank God that in our relationship with the divine we are given a choice. And how I thank God that is seems to me He wants most of all to come to us as a gentle teacher, loving Lord, and Saving grace. The choice, though, is ours.

"Murphy"

1 CORINTHIANS 4:21

Paul knows he is called and equipped to be a messenger of the Good News of Jesus, and that he works hard at sharing that message of grace. He knows how it feels to offer the word of God to an audience that seems determined not to hear or receive the Truth as their own.

He also knows that many who have heard the message, along with those who have not, have apparently chosen to use the truth to their own benefit, or to dabble in the truth only so far as it benefits them privately.

With the reminder that the faithful subscribe to the Truth for God's sake, and live their faith as a lifestyle, rather than just wise talk, he also offers those in the Corinthian fellowship a choice: you're not doing so well with the lifestyle of faith – shall I come to you as a hard disciplinarian or as a friend willing to share with you heart-to-heart?

Christ is among us of faith. It's our choice whether we invite His presence as a disciplinarian or as a friend.

REFLECTION

I remember that Mom tried to spank me once . . . she may have done so many times, but I only remember that one time, in part because it hurt so little that I laughed at her. But what impressed me most was that my laughter did not anger her. She joined me in laughter, gave me a hug, and then said, "You will always have a choice – do it right, or not. Your choice will determine whether you receive pain or joy in your heart."

Do you hold in your heart Murphy-like remembrances of hostile or hard discipline that makes you shy from anything that seems threatening, even if it's not?

Are you more inclined to be a disciplinarian or a friend to those in your circle of influence?

How has God treated you as a divine child of creation, salvation, and grace?

God's forgiveness and love are the ultimate gifts of our Creator Father. Jesus invites us to model our lives after that of the Father, and of Himself. Do you need to consider changes in your life so that you might grow in grace and be more like the Father and the Son?

Have you invited the Holy Spirit to inhabit your life and lead you in God's ways with discernment, courage, and trust?

27

"She was in the moon!"

1 Corinthians 15: 39-41
"There is an incredible glory in heavenly bodies, including the moon!"

I don't remember how many years it was after Mom died, but I'll not forget that evening when I came to grips with her sudden departure.

I suppose most of us have a pull-yourself-up-by-the-bootstraps attitude, at least here in the good old US of A, where that seems to be a motto or something. But I also suppose that in part because of that attitude we do a relatively lousy job of dealing with our grief and our pain. When something radically wrong blows up in our faces, the first thing we consider is how not to let anyone know we're flustered in the least! "I can handle it!" And off we go, burying our misery as deeply as possible, hoping that will take care of it.

At least for me, though, on this particular day I found that "handle it" practice to be a total cow-patty failure! But the benefits of that failure have paid royal dividends ever since.

The day itself had been quite a challenge. We had moved a bunch of new steers up to the northwest pasture, but they didn't want to cooperate with us, so we were all over the pastures we crossed, chasing those funky youngsters back to the herd, or pushing them to move ahead instead of turning back. It wasn't that we couldn't or didn't get the job done. It's just that it was about three times the labor we had expected, or hoped for.

At one point a crazy critter hit a fence and busted a top wire, spooking the whole bunch into a westward dash for safety. The wreck included three steers over the suddenly shortened fence, and about 55 others spread out headed toward the afternoon sun.

By the time we had gathered them back on the trail north, including the three that jumped the fence and headed east, we were at least an hour behind schedule. So we were all a bit edgy, cowboys and steers alike, and we pushed just a litter harder in the hope of finishing our work before sunset.

When we got the herd into the right pasture and shoved to water, then rode the three-plus miles back to the barn, we did so under the glory of one of God's orange, red, yellow, and blue masterpieces on the western horizon.

At that point something was stirring inside me that I had no explanation for. It wasn't until after supper, when I decided to step outside and look at the stars, that it hit me. It took me by total surprise.

I had just perched myself on the pickup hood and leaned back against the windshield to peer into the northern sky when Mom came to mind. My precious, frail, loving, give-herself-away teacher and Mom, was right there in the middle of my thoughts. And I couldn't help but cry, just a bit . . . not so anybody would notice if they happened to come join me, just a tiny bit. You know, that pull-yourself-up kind of totally out of the wherever they come from surprises kind of choke it back but roll a single tear down the cheek kind of private cries.

It didn't take me long to wonder why and to begin a self-examination of the heart. In those moments I ran the movie of my recollections by, sometimes slowly and sometimes quickly, until I came to the moment branded in my memory-bank: the last time I'd seen her alive.

It was in my parents' home in town; she was seated in the kitchen in her chair across the table from Dad. I'd dropped by for reasons long ago forgotten, and was leaving. I said bye to both of them, and as I walked past Mom toward the door I reached out with my left hand, which she took in her left hand, and for a brief moment we touched fingers. But the touch melted me all the way to my soul.

Mercy, I loved my mother! I was sad that she was so frail, and that she smoked and drank and felt compelled to stay up into all hours of the morning visiting with her wounded students. But she was a devoted Mother and teacher, and I loved her.

Then it happened – that private kind of crying, with a single tear speaking openly about the flood that could have opened up from the tear ducts if I'd not been such a tough cowboy.

I don't remember how long I sat there, leaning on the windshield, gazing into the depths of God's night-heaven. But eventually I turned to my right to get down and in so doing was surprised to find a distinctively full moon gazing right back down at me. And I swear, right there in the face of the moon, there she was, Mama, as clear as any oil portrait, but alive, and singing from Handel's work, "I know that my Redeemer liveth!"

It was then that the flood gates opened. She was in the face of the moon, singing glory to God the Creator of all of life, including that which is eternal, and there I was, cowboy boots dangling off an old Chevy pickup truck, awe-struck by the brilliance of the view, weeping like a son overcome with joy at a loving mother's embrace, again.

I slept like a contented baby that night. I'd been tucked in by the renewing of my spirit by the warmth of Mom's enduring embrace, and by the hope I cling to for eternity's joy. And finally, after these years of thinking I'd handled it, she did it for me. She was in the moon, I was in her eyes, and all was at peace.

"She was in the moon!"
1 CORINTHIANS 15:39-41

If we want a glimpse of resurrection glory, Paul invites us to look at the varieties of bodies in creation: the bodies of humans, birds, animals, fish, and even the celestial bodies of the sun, moon, and stars! In them, we catch a glimpse of the variety of beauty and brightness that inhabits the eternal. In them we catch a glimpse of resurrection's glory!

REFLECTION

I remember clearly the last moment I spent with my living mother. And I remember today as clearly as I saw it those years ago when I literally saw the face of my mother in the full moon, singing with clarity, "I know that my Redeemer liveth!"

While some may claim that I was punch-drunk from a too-hard day at work and seeing things, I believe I caught a glimpse of the awesome nature of resurrection's glory when I saw Mama's face in the moon!

Have you had a personal experience, vision or otherwise, that has solidified your faith in the eternal promises of God? Have you doubted Heaven since then?

If you have not been blessed with such assurance, how do you maintain your faith in forever? Does it help that Paul says you, and we all, can see the glory of God's forever in the uniqueness and beauty of creation?

How do you deal with the issue of death with your children? Does your simple explanation to them help stabilize your own faith?

Do Paul's assurances and invitation strike a chord of grace and peace within your soul? Have you looked for resurrection's glory lately.

She was in the moon!

28

"Busted Cinch"

Luke 2:8-14
"Don't be afraid! This is good news!"

Not everything I have claimed as my own in the cowboy realm has come to me through personal experience. Cowboys are notorious story-tellers, and sometimes well known liars! So some of what makes up my cowboy psyche has come to me in and through my own mistakes and my personal successes, but some also comes through stories, what I've been told and what I've been warned about.

The blessing in it all for me is that my total cowboy package has never stifled the creativity that my parents worked so hard to nurture and has in fact served to stimulate that imagination on many occasions. The Christmas of 2006 was one such occasion.

I rode out about a week ago to get away,
just lookin' for the gift of some prairie calm
far from the season's clamor and celebration,
and found myself more alone than I had hoped

when a frightened jackrabbit scattered out of the sage
and my bullet-proof mount bolted in surprise.

That old saddle I was in didn't fare the scare so well
when I clamped down with my thighs to hold on tight
for the cinch simply busted plumb in half,
and I found myself dumped flat on the dry dirt
lookin' up and holdin' hands full of leather
as that mighty steed took off without tack or rider!

I thought at first it'd be a long lonely walk
back to the saddle shed and warm cozy house
with all that dusty ground stretched out there
from sunrise to sunset horizon surroundin' me,
and this time was caught by stillness's surprise
when I walked into the silence I'd gone lookin' for.

By dusk the wispy winter clouds had turned red-orange,
stars were pokin' tiny holes in the creepin' purple dark,
and I found the lonesome quiet deeply deafening
until, in that solemn hush I heard 'em overhead,
way off to the eastern sky somewhere: jingles, bells,
and the unmistakable snort of tiny sleek deer.

Deer, in the sky! And they flew over quick as a flash
with a swoosh and a snort and a rein-slapped clatter,
trailin' behind 'em an overloaded tiny shiny sleigh.
And there, surprised all over again I saw him:
Santa, decked in red and white and red and jolly
waving down at me with a smile as big as that sky.

To think, all I'd wanted that day was to get away
and find some calm to settle my rattled head.
But what I found courtesy of a rabbit-busted cinch

was a Saintly Nicholas sky-born reminder
that the truest Peace of all was also delivered
on a starry silent night into a quiet Holy stillness.

"Busted Cinch"

LUKE 2:8-14

The shepherds were just minding their own business, tending to their night watch duties, when the silence was busted wide open by an angel of the Lord, then a host of angels! Not surprisingly, the surprise scared them to say the least, but they were assured of God's grace, and told the remarkably good news of the Messiah's birth!

REFLECTION

Stillness, quiet, reverie, and calm. Sometimes those times are disquieting, uncomfortable. But if given to the company of the Holy Spirit, those moments can open the heart to divine revelation, wisdom, courage, and peace. And sometimes the giftedness of that kind of stillness can be shattered with pronouncements or reminders of mercy that light up our lives!

How often do you seek a touch of the Spirit in the stillness and quiet? Where do you find that place of calm?

What has God revealed to you through those moments? How did you respond?

How blessed we are when, in the midst of minding our own business, the Lord chooses to reveal, or remind us of, divine glory! It can happen in the midst of a busy day or work or parenting as well. But when we're surprised in the stillness . . . ah, the sweet way of the Lord is indeed refreshing as the Messiah is brought to mind and heart!

Busted Cinch

"A Miracle in the Lap"

John 3:1-21
"God sent Jesus, not for God's sake, but for ours!"

I don't remember the name of the old TV western, but I'll never forget the image implanted in my mind when as a boy I saw a dirty, gruff trail hand get down off his horse and with a gentleness not seen in any other phase of his work pick up a scrawny baby calf, lay it across his saddle, and then get back on to carry the calf so it wouldn't get left behind.

It was a rescue, an act of devotion not only to a job but to a creature in need of help. I wonder today if such acts aren't a part of cowboy lore and mystique. Sure, cowboys are tough as nails and can be mean as rattlesnakes! But there are also those defining moments when a cowboy can reveal tenderness within that speaks volumes about sensitivities often deeply masked by that rough exterior.

That image was as vivid as it ever was in childhood the afternoon one early spring when we were moving cattle off winter wheat down to the ranch. These heifers had been purchased months earlier, and among the herd was one bearing an unknown surprise within, so there was a baby calf to tend. He was my surprise and responsibility since I was sent to check the northwest corner of that particular pasture.

It was abundantly clear that this maybe week old baby was weather stressed and if not for my riding up on his sleeping body might have been left behind. So I stepped off my horse, picked the calf up, laid him across my saddle, and got back up.

At that point I was deeply grateful for a gentle horse that allowed all this to take place without a rodeo, and I felt like a TV western hero! I did, that is, until the calf woke up to what was happening and became startled, frightened, and did what cattle tend to do when they get stirred up like that – all down my left pant leg, over my boot, and into the leather creases and straps of my saddle!

Thankfully it didn't take long for him to calm down a bit, the half-mile ride was without further incident, and with a wide grin the boss asked me where I'd rustled up the extra beef.

More important than all that hero cowboy stuff though was what went through my mind and heart and spirit as I rode back to the pickup. We moved slowly and carefully, giving me time to consider that infant-warm bundle astride Deuce with me. In the midst of it all I was caught up by the divine gift of the moment.

For there, in my care, was a precious creation of God, and I was a tough cowboy who had taken the time to be gentle and caring with an animal that we considered having been born to die.

At that moment I was given a lesson not to be forgotten. At that moment I realized the cowboy job was not about me but about that infant calf. It wasn't about me. It was about him.

I realized that the God of all creation and life, the God who blossomed wildflowers that might never be seen by human eyes, the God who invites us to take this human journey at least in part that so we might know a deeper measure of divine presence and grace as our own, this mighty God one day held me in His loving arms, and in looking upon me knew that it wasn't about Him. It wasn't about Him. It was about me!

Why else would the God who doesn't need us but wants us, choose to rescue all of creation by sending His Son Jesus to redeem us, and to show us the way back home?
Suddenly it became almost overwhelming to know that for each of us, held in His loving arms, God sent Jesus not because it was about God. God sent Jesus because it was about us, you and me!

With me in His arms, God said, "It's not about Me; it's about Jeff!" Holding each of us, God said, it's not about Me; it's about these, my children! With this miracle in my lap, and in His lap, the nature of my thanksgiving and praise report to the angels was transformed forever!

"A Miracle in the Lap"
JOHN 3:1-21

Sometimes the words of Jesus can seem quite confusing. But if we take the time to really listen, to question, and to believe, the truth becomes evident.

No, we cannot be born twice from our mothers. But we can indeed be born a second time by the Spirit, in faith! This possibility was made possible in the grace of God, who sent Jesus to reveal the discernable truth about divine love, that as we come to God through Christ, we might be redeemed, sustained and loved both now and forever!

REFLECTION

God soooooooooooo loved the world! God made the world for reasons we perhaps can't understand in this life, but did so with love. Here we are, God's beloved, lost, incredible children, shown the way Home in the sacrifice and victory of His own Son. It's a miracle!

Amazingly, our physical birth is about both God and us, and our Spiritual birth is about the lengths God is willing to go to insure we get back home – it's about us! When was the last time you truly felt embraced and loved by God?

In the depths of despair, or in the dances of joy, we are invited to find the Lord God present and active, loving us beyond compare. When is it easiest for you to recognize the Lord alive in your life? When is it most difficult? How can you make it easier to find Him in those tougher settings?

Is it true for you that God is most readily remembered in tough experiences? As you find Him there, are you taking notes about the divine grace your find there, for the report His angels are anticipating upon our return Home?

"True Cowboy Power"

Romans 8:18-30

"All things, ALL things great and small, done in love, count with God."

Rain can be either a curse or a blessing to a cowboy. Lightening that often comes with it is still one of the sharpest killers of the tradesmen. But rains can also bring over-busy schedules to a screeching halt, or at least change the order of priorities for a while.

That was the case one particular afternoon. The assigned task for the day included rounding up the home pasture so that we could doctor, then separating the steers into two bunches, bigs and smallers, for shipping to separate upper pastures.

The morning started out beautifully, with a fresh summer breeze and partly cloudy skies. We got the first part of the job done easily, rounding up and doctoring anything that might be sick or puny.

Things changed after lunch though, as the clouds bunched up and blew up. We were headed back to the lots to begin separating the different size steers when both Tom and I felt something odd and smelled what we later decided must have been the ozone. In that moment we froze, looked at each other, felt the hair stand up on our arms, and belly-dove for the ground!

Incredible as it was, there was no crashing thunder. There was only a blinding flash of light, and the top of a nearby cottonwood was blown to pieces. Lightening had hit so closely nearby that we sensed it in the instant before it happened, our cool
cat-quick cowboy instincts planted us nose down on the turf, and we were spared to work another day!

After retreating to the house to re-gather our courage, the rains began to fall, at times in sheets of wet, at times in gentle showers. It was decided that the sorting could wait, but other jobs needed attention.

Tom got in his pickup and headed for town to pick up veterinarian supplies, and I walked up to the machine shed. My task was the boring but necessary job of straightening out the tools and tool bench. While that may sound simple, it had been a couple of months since such attention had been given and the job was huge.

After surveying the mess I decided which part of the job I would tackle first, then second, and next and next and next! I began with the tools on the workbench so I could clear a space to work on when I addressed the tools on the floor.

The sweet smells of rain made the typically hot and dirty job more bearable, and my thoughts ranged from cow work to horse grooming, from the hay about ready for its final cutting to whether or not the rains would make water-gap repair necessary.

At one point my attention was given to the mundane

tasks in hand, the nuts and bolts from the bailer that needed to be put back in boxes, the wrenches that needed to be hung on the wall, the welding supplies that needed to be restacked in the corner. It occurred to me that while the work was mundane, it was also important.

In fact, sometimes it's the details like these that make a huge difference in a cowboy's efficiency when time is of the essence. And that's true not only of the machine shed but also of the second job facing me, straightening and cleaning the saddle shed.

So I was encouraged by the mundane and began to wonder if perhaps the discipline needed to tend to what seemed so insignificant could well define the true power of a cowboy, or a pastor, or a mother, or a carpenter, or a salesman. I began to wonder if perhaps anyone being diligently faithful to what you're equipped for and called to is the true test of a person's genuine power, strength, and integrity?

I recall a study in Romans one time when the teacher offered a simple admonition and encouragement. He said simply, "Don't let the world or your
self-centered concerns steal the joy of any given moment by keeping yesterday on your back like a load of smelly, wet manure!"

In remembering, I worked back through what I had been thinking about for the past hour while I'd progressed from the clean tool bench toward the welding stuff. I was surprised at how much of my time had been occupied in re-hashing events from the days gone by, including both the good moments as well as those moments or events that were indeed still weighing heavy on my mind.

Sure enough, I had been struggling to find the joy of

that moment's integrity, lost in a load of smelly long-gone events that nothing or nobody was requiring me to carry around any longer.

What a relief it was to reclaim the promise of faith in Paul, and to rejoice once again in the truth that nothing done in faithfulness is ever wasted. In fact, God's gentle reminder in that moment will make a powerful illustration or tone poem addition to my symphony. But for immediacy in the here and now, it also liberated me to be the powerful cowboy I was equipped and called to be in that starting-to-sparkle machine shed!

"True Cowboy Power"
ROMANS 8:18-30

O to be set free from any kind and all bondage, including the heavy stuff we carry in our past. You know: the stuff that often keeps you from stepping out through faith into a new day or a new challenge because of past fears or failures!

So we ought to unload the troubles, the sin, that we think we have to carry with us always and everywhere. It could be that the only way we accomplish that task is to remember that those challenges, when faced with truth and faith, are each parts of a greater divine whole, each valuable in its own way, and every part working together to grow us up as the children of God we are created to be!

REFLECTION

All things . . . *every* detail "in our lives of love for God is worked into something good" (Mssg)?

If that's so, God is truly a worker of miracles in my view. For some of those details have made me cringe with shame. Yet, in reviewing God's grace in spite of them, I can see that through them God has taught me lessons I could not have learned without them.

Nothing done in faithfulness, or submitted in retrospect to the mercy of God's forgiveness, is wasted. What are you hanging on to, perhaps not believing that God can or will transform it into something good that keeps you from being all that God wants you to be? How much of your thought life is trapped or stuck in the muck of past mistakes? Did you know God can, and wants to, transform your whole life experience into something valuable to you as a called and equipped person of faith?

What might it take for you to give total trust a try?

It's hard to believe that there is power in the mundane. With the world clamoring to preach and teach that power is in the glitzy and large, God's gentle grace seems helplessly impotent at times. Yet, if, IF we will take up the call of God even in the mundane, we will discover that limitless power of joy in such faithfulness. When were you last surprised by the blessing of God in the accomplishment of something simple? How has that joy become a part of the greater you, as you seek to serve the Lord with gladness?

Picking up nuts and bolts, a mess made mostly by somebody else, can seem demeaning and meaningless. But such work, done in faithfulness to God, is invaluable, and a powerful expression of life shared with the Divine. So, do it, for God's sake!

True Cowboy Power

"All-pro, DD Lewis"

1 Corinthians 10:13
"God's testing also provides resources for overcoming."

Sometimes all the smarts and experience of wily and willing cowboys can just be thrown out the window. Sometimes it doesn't matter how skilled you are. There are simply times when a practically newborn calf can confound the best of us.

Take for instance the late winter I was helping check the cows and calves in the LZ lower section west pasture. We had been fixing some fence that morning, and as it was a warmish Friday afternoon promising Spring's return, and we had worn our horses out through the early part of the week, we decided to simply drive through the pasture.

As Tom and I did so, we found a frisky young calf with a runny nose. Tom told me to drive the pickup like his roping horse, up beside the calf, and he would just rope that baby from the flatbed.

That's when the rodeo began! Three or four times I used my unquestionably expert driving skills to maneuver the three-quarter ton 4-wheel drive beast alongside the frightened calf, and each time a dead tree limb, or a cactus, or a mound of sand would throw Tom's timing off and his rope would fall just to the side, or bounce off the heels of that confounded baby.

Finally that calf grew foxier than his weeks should have allowed and he ditched us by flying down the embankment of the creek, where even this powerful pickup could not follow. Down at the dry creek bottom he stopped, looked back up at us, and – I promise – it looked as if he smiled as he turned to walk away triumphant!

By this time Tom was hostile. We needed to catch that calf so we could doctor him, and we needed to do so without running him down and making him sicker. Tom took his rope in hand and crept down a cattle trail to the creek below with the pledge to catch that crazy critter no matter what.

As I watched from atop the embankment, I saw that just as he was within roping distance, that baby saw Tom and dashed out from under his loop. I couldn't help laughing, inside where Tom couldn't hear me, as he took off on foot chasing that calf.

I followed along on the rim above and saw that the baby had spotted another trail up and away from Tom so I lay low and just as the calf dashed to the top of the rim, I pounced – I flew through the air like then Dallas Cowboy linebacker DD Lewis, with excellent form and exquisite determination, and flattened that calf as if he were a totally unaware wide receiver coming over the middle to catch a pass. I wrapped him up in a perfect tackle!

Finally, mission accomplished, and a new CB-radio handle bestowed: "All-pro!"

That week was a busy one. A light cold snow had blanketed the place on Sunday, making it look more like a wonderland than a working ranch. Hay bales were running low, so we had to buy and haul a load from the flats down to the ranch. We discovered several fences needing mending while we rode pastures alive with the year's calf crop. We had also fixed trailer springs and pickup flats almost every day.

We were persistent, though, knowing the only way to get through the week was to get through it, one day at a time. We were weary to say the least, but we were also anticipating Sunday's respite and determined to get all of our work done. And we did.

In the end the treasure for me, though, was not the accomplishment of tasks done well, or the Sunday rest, but the recognition that in keeping on keeping on we did not grow weary beyond what we could handle.

That Sunday's message was appropriate for us – even felt quite personal. The preacher said, "Isn't it amazing how God meets us at the point of need every time, supplying strength, wisdom, and courage just when most needed? Isn't it amazing how often we take that gift for granted?"

Nailed me in the breadbasket, sort of like DD Lewis might!

"All-Pro, DD Lewis"
1 CORINTHIANS 10:13

Everyone who trusts God gets God's help, no matter the nature of our testing; in His love, we can and will endure! The enduring part is the promise. The trusting part is the challenge. It all beings with that trust.

REFLECTION

At times the busy-ness of our world can get the best of

us, wear us to a wimpy wonder, and make us feel as though we've been thoroughly wasted in defeat. At other times we get a glimpse of how well we've endured, overcome, and been blessed as we find the strength to meet daily needs. In either setting, the challenge for me has always been to remember who and Whose I am, and Who offers to sustain and enrich me for the tasks at hand.

Why is it so easy to lose a vivid connectedness to God in the midst of life's busy and often noisy demands?

When was the last time you caught yourself wrapped up in the demands of a day or a specific job or a crisis of some sort and were surprised to remember that God cares, and is there with you?

When did you most recently experience a hard tackle in the hands of the world's demands? How did you respond? Did you get up and shake it off, or did you lie there dazed, not knowing what hit you?

How do you equip yourself for a new day, ready, willing and able to face whatever may come, with hope and trust and joy?

"The Old New World"

Genesis 1:1-5
"GOD created both, the light and the dark, and it was good."

In the beginning, when I was just old enough to recognize my place as a person and as one privileged to roam Wolf Creek with friends or in solitude, it felt like my whole world had been made for me.

In the beginning it was mostly about me! I wanted to be on the ranch every day. I wanted to ride a horse every time I was on the ranch. I wanted to . . . I wanted . . . I was the center of my universe.

Then one dark night I was blessed to look deep into the night sky, and as I gazed at the stars beyond counting or imagining, it began to dawn on me that maybe everything was huge beyond the limits of my vision, a vision that usually extended no further than the end of my arms or wider than the blinders I wore.

It didn't happen overnight. It took years of maturing; years in the Methodist youth group led by an angel of a teacher; years of wonder and amazement that grew in the discoveries of incredibly beautiful flowers, and silky soft baby calves, and powerfully strong and fast horses. It didn't happen overnight, this metamorphosis of my senses and my spirit.

One of the breakthroughs for me came after a day of plowing. That was perhaps the least fun labor on the ranch. Thankfully there weren't too many acres involved, but when it was time, it was time to work the ground, to plant and harvest, to weed and feed. Our favorite way to get the work done was for Tom and Jill and I to draw straws for shifts and then plow non-stop, eight hours apiece, until the whole job was finished.

I particularly enjoyed the midnight to 8, morning shift. The work was so different from usual, watching a sometimes faint marker by tractor headlight is quite different from doing the same by daylight. While it's usually difficult to hear anything but the roar of the diesel engine when plowing, it always seemed more quiet and calm and less frenetic in that darkness that led to sunrise. Those hours gave a totally different look to the world around me.

But it was what happened in the daylight of one of those shifts that helped alter my perspective and expand my perception about that beloved ranchland. One of the ways I kept awake in the heat of a plowing afternoon was to keep my eyes open as I surveyed the ground for arrow points.

For years one particular field on the lower section had been a ripe picking ground for these Native American artifacts. While I had found enough flint to fill buckets, I had never found a perfect, unbroken point, until this day. There it was, perched on a clod of dried dirt, almost waving at me for attention as I struggled to stay alert!

After stopping the tractor and climbing down, I was thrilled to pick up that perfect little point, no more than an inch from butt to tip, masterfully crafted and deadly sharp.

Then my imagination opened up full throttle and I finished plowing that field without remembering making a turn. For my wonder had transported me to a time when a hunter in this Texas panhandle tribe had taken a rough stone, flecked off tiny pieces with a larger rock, and slowly and patiently formed this point.

Maybe he had knelt beside a warm winter fire, or sat on his heels as the sun went down, and taught his son how to handle the rocks as the point took shape and then sharpen.

What was his purpose? Were there hostile tribesmen nearby that this point would be used to defeat in battle? Was this point to be aimed at wild deer or pheasant? And how did it come to be left here, unbroken and perhaps unused?

Suddenly I could see a whole village of pueblo dwellers on this field, living and working and laughing and crying together, and I became acutely aware of a time shift, of the fact that I was not the only person to have loved and worked on this creek! In truth, I felt as though I was working on holy ground. I was enjoying a sacred place because it wasn't just mine any more. It had become creation's ground.

Some years later the dating process on points like that placed their flecking at about the time this old world became a new world when Columbus sailed the ocean blue and discovered this land for me and you!

It was solidifying to think that when the first explorers and colonists set foot on our nation's Atlantic coastline, there were thriving, loving, working Native Americans on the LZ ranch along Wolf Creek, and each group oblivious to each other.

Terra firma took on a whole new meaning for me, all

mustered up through the dreaming done over a simple, small arrow point. The "world" was enlarged by centuries, and my appreciation and awe blossomed from thankfulness into amazement and wonder!

What a gift, to be one among the many whom God created in love, by love, and for love, who also had the honor of walking on brown dirt transformed into sacred ground in such recognition. What a privilege, to share with the angels how glorious it is to make that divine and eternal connection even so far from home!

"The Old New World"
GENESIS 1:1 – 2:3

In the beginning . . . God!

Not in the beginning . . . me! As much as I, and perhaps most of us, grew up thinking the world was as big as I could see and understand and no more, believing that the world was all about me, myself, and I, believing that I was the center of the universe, even more so is the truth that it's not about me at all, but about God!

REFLECTION

What a delightful shock it was that day, to be transported in spirit if not in form, to   time and place I had not known existed before that moment! I could literally imagine, and see, a whole different village than mine thriving on that ground. It was almost as if I had been blessed with a warping of time and introduced to joy in the eyes and lives of another family there on that sacred ground.

Have you considered before who else has walked the path you walk today?

Have you ever considered how much the landscape of your home stomping grounds has changed in the last 500, or 1000 years?

In considering how old your new world is, how is your view of creation affected?

Do you keep God in a too small box?

Can you let God loose in your life to be as creative in you today as God has always been in the lives of our predecessors?

Are your hopes for tomorrow altered in any way when you make connection with our ultimate past and our ultimate eternity?

33

"Mending a Washout"

Philippians 4:10-14
"Content in His strength, I can do anything He asks –
anything."

The real challenge in the mostly unpredictable Texas panhandle weather is just that: it's mostly unpredictable. A good weatherman can often suggest that conditions are becoming ripe for rain, or will remain dry as a bone. But it just seems to be beyond modern science's capacities to know when a deluge might dump itself on the desert.

The summer after one of the driest years on record, for example, was a wet surprise. The spring had been cool, with occasional showers to help wake the wildflowers and give us some hope for replenishing subsoil moisture. Little did we know to what extent that might come true.

Yet, it was no surprise when the prediction for rain was offered, and as it had happened so many times before, clouds built, moved in from the southwest up toward the northeast, and began raining only after they had passed us over. It was a soaking surprise, though, when the southwest side of that storm system rebuilt itself, actually appearing to move back toward us from the northeast.

Rain never moved in from the northeast! But rain it did, and rain, and rain, and rain. Work was washed out within an hour of the first sprinkles, roads were slippery slides within a couple more hours, gullies and draws began to trickle runoff then rush runoff toward the creek. The creek began to rise, then rage!

It would be a different world down there if the creek were a river, and a whole new world at that, cutting fully accessible pastures into a patchwork of hard to reach islands.

It turned out to be a veritable flood along Wolf Creek, not unknown but not annual either. The cleanup a few days later was a completely different kind of labor. Water gaps had been boiled open by the rushing waters, cattle had strayed from one pasture to another as if on open range, and downed tree limbs created mounds of small dams along the course of the creek.

The sight was at once awesome in recognition of Mother Nature's power, and also puzzling as we tried to assess the best response and repair. So priorities were aligned and jobs assigned and the work began.

Part of my job was working the gaps and flood trash in the home pasture. So I piled supplies in the blue pickup and headed first for the three gaps that needed to be closed so that the open range illusion could be closed to freedom-seeking cattle. Stripped to my shorts, wire and pliers in hand, into the cold running rainwater I walked.

There, as I worked to the music of rain-refreshed birds and tree leaves stirred by the breeze, it dawned on me that I myself was a part of a master concert. This particular flood

Take Me Home, Windrider

was confined to the creek, no buildings or animals were threatened or lost, and I was simply playing my part in the post-flood symphony.

The whole of the creek and its abundant life seemed washed clean. The summer air was sweet. And mocking birds sounded renewed in their chattering and singing.

It could have been so much different. The flood could have been devastating. But as it was, this flood served to wash the world clean. Yes, there was extra and new work to do. And some of our week's agenda had to be rearranged for later. But in those moments, waist-deep in home pasture water gaps, I was at peace, quite content to be accomplishing needed work while surrounded by the calm after the storm that turned out to be a blessing to my heart.

Here it was – another unique rodeo of unpredicted surprises. And here I was in the midst of it all, with a divine rainwater cold sense of peace as I closed a washed out gap, simply putting things back in their proper places.

"Mending a Washout"
PHILIPPIANS 4:10-14

. . . to be content with whatever I have. I can do all things through him who strengthens me. All things. ALL things! From the mundane to the exciting to the surprising to the deadly to the fearful to the . . . end of every day: all things can be done in divine grace!

REFLECTION

Life can often surprise us, and distress us if we're caught off guard. In a world where performance is often judged according to a schedule, such surprises can leave us with a sense of frustration, anger and/or wasted time and effort.

If Mother Nature washes out a schedule completely, nerves can become frayed as the thought of falling behind descends like a wet blanket over everything.

However, there is, there IS an alternative view. There is the view of the imprisoned Paul, who knew surprise and potential distress like I'll probably ever know. In the midst of it all, Paul found contentment, of all things!

How do you move from frustration/anger/confusion to contentment when life throws you an unexpected curve?

Is there a "contentment tool" in your box of ready response?

How does the Spirit of the Living Lord play into your making of schedules, and your hopes and dreams, and your seeking to be faithful to God in Christ?

34

"Somebody"

Ecclesiastes 7:1a
"What's in a name? Ask the Lord!"

At the Dutcher gap, things were a bit different, however. The bend in the creek there had always kept the creek deeper, and the gap was longer, and the repair work needed meant somebody had to have a helper on the creek bank and a willingness to wade neck-deep into those cold waters.

As it was, Tom was due to be a father any day, so that afternoon he came and got me from the home pasture and took me with him to the fence that separated the LZ ground from the Dutcher place.

There, he showed me how "somebody" needed to swim into the creek while he untangled the long end of the gap and threw it back across the creek as best he could. Tom was pleased to note that the "somebody" headed into the water was to be me, since Tom didn't want to get wet and risk catching a cold just before his baby was born.

Tom walked down the creek where the open gap was laid out conveniently against a huge downed tree trunk. I waded and then swam into the creek, out to a point where I thought Tom could toss the end of the gap fence, and I could retrieve it and drag it back across the creek for re-attachment to the other end of the fence.

It was then that "somebody" saw something never to be forgotten. It happened as if in slow motion, and could well have been worthy of a movie of Keystone Cops antics. For there, on that huge tree, Tom lifted the end of the fence, pulled it as tight as he could so as to increase the leverage of his throw, and swung and threw the fence as hard as he could . . . and in losing his balance, windmilled his arms while trying to balance on one leg before he flailed headlong and fully clothed into the creek!

A more delightful script or more talented stunt man could not have made for a more perfect redemption in "somebody's" mind as I choked on rainwater up to my neck laughing so hard.

Still today, the image is as fresh as it was those many years ago. The report on the other side of the comic interlude is two-fold.

First, Tom's fall was into enough water that nothing was broken, only totally soaked; and he did not catch the cold he had feared possible.

Second, I had a new name. That name was utilized frequently from that day forward. When there was a task that needed attention and "nobody" else wanted to do it, "somebody" surely would. I did.

Still today I wear that name with pleasure. It became an identifying symbol of my willingness to tackle most anything. It's a lot better than some of the other names I could have been called! It was a special treat the day M.F.'s sister was visiting and I, shirtless on a warm afternoon, was introduced to her as "somebody." She smiled and said, "Yep, that's sure some body!"

My ranch name: hmmm. Could it perhaps be worth a Canon in b-major-humble?

"Somebody"
PROVERBS 22:1

What's in a name? A good one is more valuable than all the riches of this world! I like Rocky, or Samson, or The Duke. Apparently, though, even Sue and Slim and Bob are more valuable than all the world's riches if they belong to the faithful.

REFLECTION

I remember with a twinge of sadness how we used to, as kids, call each other names. Sometimes those names were shouted in defiance, or screamed as taunts. At other times they were meant to be descriptive, or even complimentary.

Every once in a while such a name, offered for whatever reason, stuck with the kids to which they were thrown. I remember Bobby never forgave the fact that when he was once called "Beany" because he was skinny as a green bean, it stuck for two or three years. Then he literally outgrew it, he got big, and he was tough enough to put the name to rest, so we called him Bob!

It's also true that the names we've been given can take on special meaning by the way in which we live. They reflect our nature so that when our name is spoken, a certain picture is drawn in the minds of the hearers. One such name is *Jesus.* When that name is spoken, every person of faith can see in the mind's eye a picture of how you believe he looked, or see him preaching or healing or dying. Truly, as the songwriter claimed, "There's just something about that name!"

How about you and your name? What does your name, or even your nick-name represent to you? What do your friends and family think of when your name is spoken?

How do you *hope* people respond at the mention of your name!?!?

Is your name a valuable asset to you in your faith and faithfulness, or have you even thought about it before?

Ultimately, though, how do you think the Lord God responds when your name is spoken to Him?

"A Bloody Encounter"

James 1:16-18
"Remember, everything good comes from God."

As it seemed to happen too often in the heat of summer, it came my turn to drive the tractor again. We were working the ground just across the road from the house at the Lower Section, hoping this might be the final plowing before the wheat was planted.

Jill had worked on part of the ground the day before and parked the tractor right near the house. After breakfast I simply walked out, water jug in hand, belly full of pancakes and scrambled eggs, making mental preparations for the work.

Oil had to be checked, fuel added, everything hit with the grease gun, the normal kinds of maintenance and watch-care before starting up. I even wondered if I might find an arrowhead since it fell to me to plow the ground richest in those hidden treasures.

But as I got to the tractor, fully intending to open the cab and place my water there before servicing everything, I was put on full, muscle-tensed, nerves on alert, ready to spring out of harm's way mode by the disquieting buzz of a rattler.

The old man was coiled in the shade of the tractor exactly below the little ladder that led to the cab, precisely where I needed to step in order to begin my day's work. It was his spot, and he was intent on sticking to it. Any doubt I may have had vanished in the distinctive buzz of that warning-tail: he was going nowhere of his own accord!

Now, most of the time I'm content to live and let live when it comes to those nasty rattlers out in the pasture. Typically they're a tough bunch, hard to kill, and a challenge to run off. I usually let them be. However, when they're this close to the house where children of all ages, and precious grandchildren roam free, each of us adults does whatever is necessary to dispose of the crawly critters, permanently.

That was the task at hand for me in that moment. I made a quick survey of the grounds, spotted a hefty dead tree limb, retrieved it, and mapped out my strategy. I planned to move the limb toward the rattler, let him strike at it, and then quickly stab down on him right behind his head with a deadly and merciful blow.

He had other ideas though, for when I moved that limb in close he dodged it and struck out at my boot instead! I was surprised but not convinced that I ought to leave him alone, so I jumped out of his strike path and positioned myself for another try.

The second attempt was very much like the first, with the same results, only this time, after almost making contact with me, he decided to take the battle to the source of contention and charged me with intention.

My heart was at this point racing, way up around my ears, and I made a mad dash for the plow. I jumped up there like a well-conditioned athlete, turned with that stout stick to defend myself, and found that rattler trying to slither up a plow-blade shank after me!

The battle was now in full fledged flail as I beat him back, thrust the stick at his head, dodged another strike attempt, and tried desperately not to miss a step on the deck of that plow.

Finally I guess he'd had enough, for he grabbed my weapon out of my hands, jabbed me in the stomach, and hollered, "Take that, you cowboy cad!"

Pushed to my limits, that was the straw that broke the tummy skin. I grabbed the stick back and finally dealt the deadly blow, ending this dance of nerves and anger for good.

At least that's the story I told M.F. when I went back to the house to wash the river of sweat from my face and drink from a bottle of cold Gatorade before heading back. In truth, the stick broke at one point, bounced back into my midsection drawing blood, and made me angry enough to finish the job.

The rattle itself counted eight rings, and had obviously been broken off at its end. That snake was old, wise and tough as a boot. Now the danger of his presence was long gone, children and cowboys alike were safe, and I was a half hour behind schedule.

But the schedule was also lost in my imagination and wonder. What kind of snake did Adam and Eve face? Did they not know the danger possessed within his wiles and ways? Or did they not understand yet the grace and the also the discipline of the Father? And why did God create such critters anyway?

If nothing else, my encounter with that rattler on that particular day led me to consider again the glory of God's love for me, to receive again James' encouragement that we remember there is absolutely nothing deceitful in or about God, to give thanks that in the midst of it all the Holy Spirit was present to remind me of God's care, to renew my faith and gratitude, and perhaps even to guide my steps in safety and the possible avoidance of another unforgettable bloody encounter.

"A Bloody Encounter"
JAMES 1:16-18

There is nothing deceitful in God, whose purpose in creation was that we might be a first fruits of grace. First fruits: like the earliest to ripen – the fruit that pays the most attention to the food on the table and grows up quickest, right?

REFLECTION

Rattle snakes are, like most snakes, amazing creatures. The way they move, sometimes very quickly across the ground on their bellies, can surprise you. And that rattle: what a perfect signal to broadcast when there is need to warn the world that this snake is on alert and ready to defend territory!

In its own way, the potentially deadly, and painfully defensive rattle snake is a wondrous work of creation. Truly, there was nothing deceitful in God's creation of the snake. But they are a wild critter, and we humans run deep risks if we think we can live in peace with them all the time.

It just seems true to me that in all of life there are circumstances or situations or conditions that challenge us to a point of critical decisions. Will we step up in faith and walk away from obvious danger? Will we risk walking away from God's will by choosing the way of the world?

Or can we find, even in the bloody encounters of life,

evidence of God's creative genius and Holy Spirit presence? Where is the glory in those frightful experiences that we get to report to the angels when we get back home?

Do you often feel like first fruits of God's grace in moments of distress? Can you? How?

A Bloody Encounter

36

"It's not free!"

Psalm 146
"Thank God, God is Lord and I am not! Hallelujah!"

If you've been there you know that cowboy work may seem glamorous on the silver screen, but it's much more gritty than glamorous in reality. Whether riding pastures, branding and doctoring, feeding hay in the winter or hauling hay in the summer, building or fixing fence, a cowboy works dirty and hard most of the time!

But the work of the cowboy holds rich rewards as well. It's my gut feeling that cowboys are some of the best among us at finding evidences of a living God no matter where their work may take them. I promise, some of those places raise a sweat that's far less than sweet.

However, with a sensitivity that is born and nurtured under the tall sky as your roof, and the wondrous dirt earth as your dance floor, it's perhaps true that a cowboy knows more about God's waltz than the on-looking outside world might suspect.

That wisdom comes at a cost though. And the price is

paid both early and late, with little rest between!

The sun rose too early this morning, as did I in hasty response.
There's work to be done and no doing it except by muscle and sweat.
So I gulped down the steamy coffee that smelled so much richer than it tasted,
threw down the half-cooked eggs, jumped into my chinks and boots
and slipped out the squeaky back screen door.

It was too early, but my how the dew-spangled ground
was freshly damp and cool and clean!
And the horses, they needed me – needed me to feed them.

Chores quickly completed with confidence,
I threw my saddle over the trusty buckskin
and off we went, out to check both cattle and fence,
north pasture, middle pasture, home pasture.

On the ride back from the north I mused at the deep late morning sky
and wondered, "How's the Lord with all of this?"
I wondered about my love of this job and place,
and about His love of me, here and now.

It occurred to me that this hard life is at times like bitter lemons
that have to be tamed with water and sugar before I can enjoy them.
I mean, cowboyin's tough, but the rewards are rich and sweet too
in satisfaction, a healthy night tired, and anticipation for

tomorrow.

Surely that's the way with the Lord and my amazing Savior:
as I pledge myself and all I am and have to Him,
and labor in uncompromising trust whether in a saddle or on
the ground,
I'm blessed with divine contentment and assurances of peace
even as I consider how it must be done all over again at
sunrise.

But such grace is not mine for nothing – it's not free.
Sometimes the morning seems to come too early,
yet when the Risen Son welcomes me with loving and open
arms
and the pledge of His guidance, protection and courage,
my rising to meet Him is made divine joy in His rising to
meet me.

"It's not free!"

PSALM 146

Put your hope in God Almighty, for God alone is God,
and God always does what He promises to do! Always! The
challenge is to know what the promises are.

REFLECTION

I've known many a morning when I didn't want to get
out of that bed. I've known many an evening when that bed
was hit too late because of rodeos that stretched it way beyond
sunshine. I've known many a frozen winter morning when the
warmth under the blankets was more powerful than the smells
of multi-grain pancakes and bacon!

I've also known many a day when, after forcing myself

to rise, I was rewarded with reminders of Jesus' first Rising for me! God promised to save us, and me, and it's been done. God promises to gift us with wisdom and courage, and even though it may not always look like it in the middle of an unexpected bronc ride, it takes cowboy smarts to know when to hang on tight and when to let go!

Most of all, though, if a person falls in love with the hard work of a cowboy out in the open spaces of a ranch, there are moments when all the drudgery and forced rising falls quickly away as a tiny rabbit dashes out from under a bush, or a majestic hawk circles in the coolness of the morning's mist, or a horse makes a perfect cut on a stubborn steer, or a sunset lights a fire on the horizon. In those moments cowboys are invited to remember who and Whose they really are, and to celebrate God's tender loving care in promises fulfilled.

When was the last time you were caught up in a troubling or difficult day and found yourself totally surprised by evidence of God's presence right there in the middle of it all?

Are there things you can do to help insure your awareness will be keen throughout any given day, so that you're open to the proof that your rising in the morning was worth the effort?

Has the Risen Son recently reminded you that no matter the difficulty of your labors, nothing compares to the sacrificial nature of His? When did His Rising most recently bless you in response to your own?

"Out to Pasture"

James 3:13
"Let your life of faith be offered with wise gentleness."

I don't spend in inordinate amount of time remembering or dreaming about my days as a full-time cowboy. But it's amazing to me how often my days as a pastor bring to mind the cowboy lifestyle.

The counseling I do sometimes reminds me of riding a bucking horse. While I've only done that a few times, some of those who come before me seeking help, seeking "the wisdom of my years," as one friend called it, is tough stuff. It seems that daily we all face moments if not hours of a rough ride in relationships, in job settings, in goal attainment.

At times we are also challenged by fulfilling responsibilities and find ourselves out there alone, taking care of the details one item at a time, one after another, and hanging in there until the job is finished, sort of like the rote details and chore of fence building, or mending.

Sometimes we sweat with hard labor, or with concern, or with fear, both in life apart from ranching, and in the cowboy world. And when the going is most difficult we might even wonder if we'll survive, and perhaps through it all we long for rest, or even for retirement.

I remember when Jill told me that Deuce had been put out to pasture. It was both a sad and honorable moment for me. I was sad that my favorite cow pony of all time had grown old enough that he was too old for the hard work of the ranch life. But it was also honorable because it meant another of the well loved LZ ranch horses, this remarkably gentle partner, had earned rest from his labors and the blessing of open ground to graze his final years through.

He had fought the good fight, as they say, had come out a winner, and was rewarded by being put out to pasture.

There used to be a place on the ranch where old pickups and trucks and tractors and combines and fence posts and electric fence wire and barbed wire and tires and wheel bearings and tools and all sorts of other such stuff was dumped, just laid aside, put out to dirt.

Can you imagine the stories each of those old used up items could tell?

A busted wheel bearing on the 18-foot stock trailer for example: "I can't believe you expect me to hold up on this rough pasture ground, you crashing through weeds and ruts with my trailer overloaded, in too big a hurry to get this job done so that you can move on to another job that doesn't need to be done so fast!"

A short roll of rusty old barbed wire maybe: "Why in the world are you rolling me up like you'll ever intend or want or need to use me again? Why don't you just toss me in the trash draw where I can rest in peace, instead of being cursed to hope or wonder when you might come for my help?"

With age, Deuce got wiser and better at working with cows. He learned how to read a cow's intention or dream and how to hold them or cut them with ease. The more I rode him the more I appreciated that accumulated wisdom, and our trust of one another. His pasture was thick with healthy buffalo grass and the promise of alfalfa in the lean months. Being put out in his pasture was a gift of honor, and respect, and gratitude.

I've wondered before: what'll folks do with me when I'm done for? Have I been gentle? Do I possess wisdom? I've wondered before: has my life merited dirt, or a rich pasture? I'm anticipating a divine answer beyond my imagination, and I'm certain my return home will create in me a glorious postlude to my symphony!

"Out to Pasture"
JAMES 3:13

The work of a good horse is, in part, guided by the bit in its mouth. God uses the bit of "salvation" in us, and guided by that gift it is possible for us to live with gentleness born of wisdom.

REFLECTION

It seems that the goal is to live a good life. In this world such a goal would be pursued in the hope of attaining, earning or receiving the accolades and compensation due a job well done.

Not of this world, however, in faith, such a goal would be pursued in view of God's best hope of each of us, without reference to rewards or earnings. It would be pursued perhaps to make it plain to the world that we belong to the One who taught us how to live like that.

Isn't it amazing how, even when it's not our primary aim that living this life with gentleness born of wisdom invariably brings its own reward: contentment in the Christ? What more could we ask for beyond that eternal joy?

What have you done with gentleness today that brings you that contentment? How have you utilized your wisdom for goodness sake?

We come from dirt and return to dirt, but live forever in the lush graces of our eternal Home. Do we have to earn that promise?

"The Misguided Mama"

Joshua 1:9; John 10:1-5
"What are you afraid of? GOD is your companion and guide!"

Looking back now I find it kind of humorous, and I sort of understand. Back then it was both fun to have the task, and aggravating when it didn't get done! I suppose that's just the way it is with a misguided mama.

I mean, all we wanted to do was gather a pasture of cows and calves and move them from a summer of grazed down buffalo grass into an adjoining pasture that had laid empty for a year so that they would have abundant fall grazing heading into winter! But it never failed – there was always at least one misguided mama in the bunch who thought it would be better to run, duck, and hide with her calf.

Now I understand the protective instinct involved, and I might do the same in some circumstances, but old #42 had been on the ranch for seven years now and was as stubborn this day as she was when she birthed her first calf! Surely she should know that, yes, on a rare occasion we would doctor and spray, but most of the time we were just moving her to better grass, right?

I've wondered if she knew all this, and just chose to make life a challenge for me because she was a tease! It really never bothered me, except when Tom or Lawrence was in a hurry, or a storm cloud was bearing down on us and I was in a hurry as well. Other than that, I enjoyed reigning Deuce out in pursuit of her escape attempt, and letting that incredibly talented athlete round, confront, turn, and nudge her back to the herd. All I had to do was hang on and enjoy the ride!

The last full year I was on the LZ ranch I chased down #42 one more time. It was a pleasure, but it also gave me pause. I wondered if her choice to make a mad dash for freedom, as misguided as it was, might not be symbolic of a friend of mine.

I'll hold his name in confidence to protect the guilty, but his actions were sort of like those of old #42. It seems that every time he found a new job he would last about three or four months and then would start to feel hemmed in, so he would duck and run. He'd quit and go searching for another job.

It was as if he lacked a sense of security amidst the frailties of this life, in the swirl of situations and choices that each of us face on a daily basis. But I'll never stop wondering why he thought he was finding any sense of direction or comfort in his drinking and womanizing.

He looked for all the world to me like a misguided, or unguided, or disconnected young man of misery. He looked and acted lost most of the time. He needed a steady, sure, and secure shepherd to show him the way to fulfillment and contentment.

Known by God before he was born, invited to this human experience so that he might discover what it's like to find God in the midst of a sojourn away from home, I wondered when my friend became disconnected from that plan. And I wondered how he might ever reconnect if somebody didn't intervene.

Could I, I wondered, ride out ahead of him and let the Holy Spirit, my Windrider, round, confront, turn, and nudge him back toward home?

Could I inquire about his history with the Messiah, or lack thereof, and have the knowledge, wisdom, and courage to share with him my history?

Could I step out in the mystery of my own faith and experiences with the Spirit of the Living God and invite him to join me along the way?

If I cared enough about a misguided mama we called old #42, could I care enough about my friend to do any less for him than I did for her time after time after time?

Could I invite him to know my trusted Shepherd as his own, and invite him to follow with me?

"The Misguided Mama"
JOSHUA 1:9; JOHN 10:1-5

The command was simple: be strong and courageous, for God is with you no matter where you go. That will always be true so long as we follow the one true Shepherd, whose voice we know without doubt. Him we can follow without fear.

How do we discern the difference in His voice and the multitude of others crying out our name and asking for help? What constitutes a valid cry? Then again, if we're focused on the Shepherd's voice alone, I suspect we hear no other.

REFLECTION

Life was always mellow for me, as much as I can remember. I was pretty much a good kid, I didn't like being in trouble, I enjoyed it when my parents approved of my actions, and I liked friends who liked me.

Then I came to Christ as a teenager, without reservation or hesitation, but wondering how the Messiah could make my life any better than it was! Mercy, what a delight it has been to have my eyes opened to how not-nice I could be and sometimes I was before I came into the Shepherd's fold. It was amazing to me how I could see Him out there, even before I knew Him, gently inviting me to get acquainted.

Since that time I've often looked back with thanksgiving, and almost daily have found reasons for rejoicing that it is Him I follow. Where there is so much anguish and anger and angst in this world, there is a peace that passes all reason or understanding in my heart. I no longer live for approval: I live for Him, though imperfectly, yet finding my peace in the sound of His guiding voice.

There, following the Messiah, I live with divine wisdom and courage, knowing He will never ever lead me astray, and always and ever lead me a step closer to home.

My personality is genuinely shy. Is that the only reason I hesitate at times to speak of my faith and my Savior? Or am I afraid of something?

Grateful to the brim for the question once asked of me, "Knighton, when are you going to ask Jesus to be Lord of your life?" why would I ever hesitate to ask that question of anyone else?

What is it that most frequently gets you off track in your desire to be faithful?

Who or what is it that you trust most in this life? Where are you going? Do you dread the day, or celebrate with abandon?

"R&R Owie!"

1 Thessalonians 5:16-18
"This is God's will: rejoice with grateful unending prayer."

It wasn't very long ago that my well had been running a little dry, I decided it was time for a change of scenery/routine and chose to take a 3-day break, head for the LZ ranch of my lifetime adoration and labors, and seek reconnection with Mother Earth to refill my spirit a bit.

I went to the ranch on a Thursday, Friday, Saturday for some R&R and labor that shows immediate evidence of productivity or not (so much different from ministry's day to day), slept from 9:30 Thursday night until 6:30 Friday morning without rolling over, and felt truly refreshed in body and soul when I woke.

I walked down to the creek just as the sun came up and went fishing. In 35 minutes I had landed four very nice eating size bass that I shared with LZ creek friends at a delicious suppertime of food and fellowship that evening.

The lower section had been trashed by a creek flood a couple of months earlier, and I was enjoying cleaning up some of the damage left in the yard later that morning when I planted my booted left foot on a nail that went through that sole like a hot knife through olive oil (Remember, I was refreshed and at the top of my awareness, strength and agility!) That set me up to doctor my blood-gushing self, then put the boot back on and continue cleaning up the remains of the east wall of the saddle shed that the creek deposited against an immovable cottonwood. Tough cowboy that I used to be, I worked through the day, limping without reservation, until the job was done.

I traveled home to Kansas earlier than I had planned on Saturday because there was no way I could put my swollen foot in a stirrup and ride like I had hoped to do that afternoon. But the trip was not wasted because with my wounded foot on ice I managed that shared supper with friends, and the next morning got a good start on a great book titled "Misquoting Jesus" about the history of how we got the Bible, and the scribes who wrote it down, and how they "may" have changed a thing or two to suit their own interpretations (nothing new under the sun today). This book ought to be seminary required reading.

It amazed me how things work out: the schools of cowboy safety and biblical scholarship were an unusual but delightful classroom combination that might not have been attended without the former inviting the latter with such painful insistence. So, should I be glad I stepped on that nail?

Back in Kansas, I headed to the health department Monday morning to satisfy the nine loving mother-hens in church Sunday who threatened to come get me and take me if I didn't promise to go get a tetanus shot, even though my most recent was still recent enough. Because I didn't want a 9-lady escort I went by myself, like a good cowboy should! Besides all that, I was extremely glad to have been blessed with strong bones because the swelling was down enough Monday morning that I could surmise that if the nail had not landed squarely on the bone of my first toe in from the little toe, it would have forced its way completely through my foot and I would have had a different problem than just a well-doctored puncture wound and bruised bone to deal with, so I'm grateful for strong cowboy bones!

Into the new week I hobbled forward with the hope of quick healing and fully-weighted walking, tended to by the gracious care of the Spirit refreshment received at the ranch. I was also blessed by the surprising experience of being reminded that God is attentive to our every need, including the blessing of cowboy owies that confirm the value of the confidence and competence born of unwavering faith. There is grace in God's presence and every circumstance! Every grace is worthy of prayerful thanksgiving.

"R&R Owie!"
1 THESSALONIANS 5:16-18

Pray always, consciously and in the spirit, giving thanks IN all circumstances and situations and rodeos and injuries, not FOR them all.

That's so much easier said than done, especially after an unplanned rodeo that knocks you for a loop. But that's the way of the Kingdom. Isn't it worth at least a try?

REFLECTION

Situations and circumstances have a way of deflecting the attention from that place the attention had been focused, and can do so suddenly, without warning, and at times very painfully. What's the first move for a person of faith, after the shock, surprise, scream (if needed) wears off?

Always? Pray and rejoice always? Does that mean in all ways also?

How do you do it – what do you do that lets God know you are rejoicing? What is rejoicing anyway? Can you do that always?

What are the mechanics of prayer in your life? Or, is prayer a mechanical thing that can be described? Better perhaps: what are the rituals, or the conscious aspects of how you pray?

This is God's will for us. How much weight does the will of God bear in your life?

What difference does it make when you obey God's will . . . really, the true discernable difference?

"Signs of Life"

John 10:7-13
"Trust him. He has laid down his life for you!"

The first time I remember encountering death my grandmother told me simply, death is a part of life. It took a lot of years for that funny sounding reference to make any sense to me. After all, my cousin and I were lamenting the death of a dog that had been run over by a car. It seemed so final, an end unto itself.

As I matured in age and wisdom, though, I could see some of what Grandma was saying. I first noticed the truth in her mysterious message on the ranch, where even as a boy I became fascinated by acres and acres of wildflowers, brilliant and varied colors that seemed to explode so soon after the melting of the gray skies and plain white snow-covered pastures.

The winter had felt like a time of dying and death, shrouded in constant cold. Then the spring scattered that shroud with a tapestry of vibrant Indian blanket, wine cups, and sunflowers.

Age helped me to grow accustomed to the season's cycle, to endure the harsh parts of winter in hope of spring's surprises, and to suffer summer's heat in the promise of fall's refreshing cool.

Then, some years later, Deuce died. Again years later Snips died. Between the death of those two talented and trusted horses, Grandpa Dee died. Then Grandpa Dan died. Then Mom died, then Gammy, then Grandma, and finally Dad.

Yet every spring before, between and after, there was that multi-colored tapestry to remind me that death was not the end of anything. It was, as my mother used to tell us, the ultimate graduation! Death is simply that given time when all things are welcomed, as they cross the royal graduation stage, to receive a divine welcome home.

I'm guessing now, but I believe that if I had not been blessed in my early years with such words of comfort and insight as Grandma and Mom offered with their own amazing brand of grace, I would have missed the tiny but brilliant reminders I found a few years back.

I had been invited to attend a springtime LZ family reunion, to renew friendships and share the wonderful memories we grew up in and through. I went to the ranch and was almost blown away by the loving reception. I am still incredibly gifted by the reflections and remembrances we shared. It had been several years since I had seen many of those among that extensive clan, and it was almost like resurrecting a joy that had withered with time, giving it new life all over again.

The abundant happiness of that renewing experience was then topped off as I walked around the corner of the house. I don't know if they had been planted there by M. F. or if

Mother Nature had performed yet another miracle, but there, growing up through the empty spaces in an old weather-washed cow skull was a small collection of tiny red, white and red/white flowers.

Emerging from the perfectly distinct reminder of death was a promise of new life! In that favor of recognition I was given another reminder that in such signs of life I am (we are) offered reasons for rejoicing.

We are on a journey home, and the path is marked all along the way in the constancy of changing seasons, by birth and death, through agony, grief, and comfort, in wonder and assurance, and with simple, tender signs of life. Ah, if we but have eyes to see!

"Signs of Life"
JOHN 10:7-11

The Good Shepherd, who is the "gate" in the keep, is the only Shepherd who promises, without hesitation or reservation, life and life abundant, no matter what, both now and forever.

Forever? How long is that? When does it begin? I suppose such a promise is made only to those who pay attention to the Shepherd's work as the gate!

REFLECTION

Abundant life: that which is lived in the assurance that this is not all there is to it, and that in Christ the "what's next" can remain unknown and yet also exciting to consider. After all, if the Shepherd has proven a capacity for protecting us sheep, why would we ever doubt our ultimate outcome?

Makes me wonder why cows are so darned ornery, or

heifers are so skittish and single-mindedly crazy! After all, I'm just trying to keep them safe . . . until they face their ultimate outcome!

If I was beef on the hoof, I'd fight for my freedoms too! Thank God, though, I'm not meat being fattened for the dinner table. I am, and we are, beloved children of our gracious God, who promises the protection and guidance of a perfect Shepherd, who wants nothing less than to see us get home, safely.

When was the last time you felt like beef on the hoof for a boss or a job? How did you handle those feelings?

When was the last time you simply counted the blessing of remembering and accepting the truth, that you are a beloved child of God?

How deeply do you trust our Shepherd – totally, somewhat, not at all? Why or why not?

"A Wispy Wind-born Reminder"

Ephesians 1:3-14
"Adopted as we are, the praise of His glory is our life's joy!"

At that particular moment I didn't want anyone trying to sooth the savage beast stomping around inside of me. I had had a thoroughly bad day, even though a bad day as a cowboy was better than the best day I'd had in any other endeavor to that point.

The whole day had seemed to be a total bust. Nothing I had set out to do got done without a riot of comical errors or a botched bundle of stupid mistakes. Nothing, absolutely nothing had been done easily.

Now I know life's tough, it never seems really easy. But I don't remember another day when *everything* had been so tough. I mean, sure there were days when hay bales fell off the truck and exploded on the roadside, and cattle out needed to be put in, and the horses were plain lethargic. But even in those days there was something that went right, that redeemed the effort it took to rise before the sun and take a stab at being an efficient cowboy. Even in those worst days there was a perfectly stretched fence wire, or a cool breeze to offset the fact it was time to plow!

But not this day. Not this scorching summer day after the annual 4th of July picnic. I couldn't even pick up the fireworks trash without reaching down for an expended bottle rocket and also coming within inches of grabbing a baby rattler by the snout! While I'd fixed many a broken fence wire, never before had a new stretch busted loose from the corner post, twice!

The dependable blue pickup also decided this was the day to blow a belt; and the day we went for the horses and found that someone had left the gate open so there was no horse in the barn to ride out on and gather the others; and the day I slipped in a fresh cow patty and fell smack dab rump down on a cactus; and the day that MF ran out of ketchup before supper was served; and on and on and on.

What a miserable, rotten, forgettable day it was – until: until I was walking back to the corral to unsaddle and feed Deuce. The sun was on its way to nightfall, a gentle and cooling breeze was tickling my face, and for whatever reason I looked up.

What a gift it was: a single, small, wispy puff of orange-kissed white wandering wind-born across the horizon and it's backdrop of a deep and darkening expanse of summer sky and approaching sunset.

There, at the near close of what I thought I had experienced as a thoroughly forgettable day, was a divine reminder that in the midst of it all, I was not alone. In fact, in the miracle of that single puff of moisture riding across the sky, God gave to me an assurance that I'll never forget.

Because of that gift I'll also remember that particular

day with reverence. For there, framed by blue on what seemed a rotten day was the reminder that down to the intricate details, God had me, and us, in mind when that colorful reminder was painted upon that divine canvas.

Stopped dead in my tracks, I was filled with awe and thanksgiving at the sight, and at the realization that the humongous challenges of the day were now done for. In that moment I was awash in peace beyond my understanding, but not beyond my receiving. I knew that tomorrow would be a blessed day as well.

"A Wispy Wind-born Reminder"
EPHESIANS 1:3-14

Destined, by God's good pleasure, God's choice, God's will: adopted, belonging, protected, and blessed with a perfect inheritance to anticipate, and gifted with a Holy Spirit capacity for living each moment of each day as a gift worthy of praise!

That's me, and you! Can you believe it? It's true no matter what the day may bring . . . moment by moment!

REFLECTION

It's so very easy to get lost in the busy-ness and the challenges of living in a lost world. It's so very easy to slip beneath the waves and wish for a simple drowning to end the pain. It's so very easy to wish for a lightning bolt to bring it all to a quick-fried conclusion.

But then again, that's not God's desire or design. If I'm right, about the invitation to live apart from Home for a little while and to collect evidence of grace even here, so that an angel-report can be compiled upon our return, isn't it those moments of trial and challenge and pain that offer us the truest sight or glimpse or reminder of grace? Aren't those moments so much more valuable as treasure amidst the junk than those we find handed over on a silver platter?

How amazing it is when there, suddenly, in the simplest of simple ways, we see a brilliant, poorly-disguised sign of God's attentive care and offering of grace. Now THAT'S cool, to say the least.

"Who's running this place?"

Ephesians 2:8-10
"We are what God has made us to be: saved by grace."

I can remember that afternoon as if it happened yesterday. I can also remember my remorse at having opened my mouth! For at the time it seemed to have done more harm than good.

As I recall, it was in the late fall, after we had brought in the last load of alfalfa from the hay field. We were all tired, as that work had a way of wearing us out. But the work had gone smoothly, and we'd had a weekend to recuperate.

We gathered that evening at High Loper's request. He wanted us to visit about how the ranch was working, to brain storm how we might get our work done more efficiently, and to dream about how we might make the work more enjoyable. After supper we sat together in chairs outside under the gigantic oak in the front lawn.

The light breeze was cool and refreshing. It was coming off the haystack, so it was kissed by the smell of sweet alfalfa. We were relaxed and in good spirits.

Our conversation was mostly simple, with much

affirmation, lots of joking and ribbing going around, and a dash of serious wonder thrown in for consideration. Most of the specific words are now long gone from my brain's memory banks. But I will never forget the only serious word I spoke.

I considered its offering carefully, almost didn't say anything, and after I spoke I immediately felt I had spoken out of turn. The silence among us was almost deafening enough to cover the whisper of a breeze in the leaves overhead. All I had said to Tom was, "I wish it was possible for you to run the ranch, instead of you're letting the ranch run you."

I am to this day not sure where that remark came from. Yes, it's true that about a week earlier we had a chance to take a day off and go to town, but the threat or hope of rain kept us at it. For a while it angered me because all we were doing was scooping the dried manure from twelve years of no attention out of the home corrals!

The front-end loader on the tractor was filled time and time and time again with the, well, the fertilizer, which was then scattered in the horse pasture. Where the tractor couldn't go, 12-14 inches of the manure had to come out one hand shovel scoop at a time.

The work was not terribly tough, but there was a lot of fertilizer to move, so the work went on and on and on. It did get a bit nasty when a wind would whip around a barn corner, blow up a tiny tornado of dry stuff into the face and eyes, and plug up the sinuses instantly. But all in all, it was just plain old hard work, the kind of work that most ranch work happens to be.

Perhaps a week before that, when another threat of rain kept us doing the lowly plowing through a weekend, the ranch seemed to be in charge. Punching cows in an emergency, or to avoid weather threats, was one thing, but I didn't think riding the tractor was ever worth giving up a weekend for!

Then there were the two endless days of cleaning up the machine shed, during the two days when it did happen to rain without warning.

It just seemed to me that at times it could become a grind, rather than good work that we cherished and enjoyed. Maybe I wasn't getting enough time in the saddle, or I hadn't taken advantage of what little time off we got that fall. Whatever it was, I had apparently had my fill, and my weariness bubbled over in frustration that I verbalized as though I were an authority.

In these years since then, though, I have realized it was a good question, even though it was a hard one to hear, and a hard one to work through at that moment. Now I understand that I had also distressed those whom I worked with when they couldn't tell from my demeanor or my labors or my words just who was in charge of running my life! That was nobody's fault but my own.

I mean, we all know that fertilizer happens, especially on a ranch with 300 mama cows and calves, a dozen or more horses, and a couple thousand yearlings on winter wheat. It just happens, no matter who's running the place. Sometimes life demands that it be cleaned up.

Truth be known, the glory of God in the midst of the fertilizer, no matter who's in charge of running the ranch, is still there for the celebrating! I did enjoy almost all of the work of a ranch hand, and remembered the blessed presence of the Creator in the midst of those labors most of the time.

But it always seems to be a challenge to remember, then to claim the glory in the gift of good work, and in doing that work with integrity. When I'm able to do that, to let the Holy Spirit nudge and remind me, and then to celebrate the gifts in hand, I need never ask who's running the place because in those moments I know. In those moments I gather refrains of praise for the symphony under construction, directed by the Maestro's hand.

"Who's running this place?"
EPHESIANS 2:8-10

We are created by God's hand and desire, and are saved by grace through One willing to die to insure our eternal destination. We boast in nothing ourselves but live in gratitude that produces good works that honor God and bless one another. How amazing and incredible and marvelous is that?

By God's own design we have both meaning and purpose in this life. As we collect evidence of God's abiding presence to us and leadership of us, we gather bits and pieces for our grace report upon our return Home. Ain't God smart?!?!

REFLECTION

This world is just simply in your face all the time! We can't escape that fact. But we can be blessed when we remember that such is not necessarily a sign of power, of divine power to be submissive to. The other power, the Atonement power of God, is also there, though not so noisy or irritating or pushy. This other power, truthfully the only real power in the universe, is inviting rather than demanding, and gracious rather than cocky.

So why is it so hard to give sway to that divine power of God? Why is it so challenging to say NO to the world and YES to the Lord?

Why is it so easy to get caught up in the immediacy of the world's busy stuff, and so hard to remember "this is not all there is to it"?

Come, Holy Spirit, lead us to a new way of listening, counting divine blessings, and honoring the Lord with our attentive trust!

Who's running this place?

"Counting on One thing and One thing only!"

Luke 10:38-42

"Don't be distracted. Focus on one thing only."

He was there one day, and the next he was gone. I'd known it many times. It's a part of what happens when working with horses. Sometimes they get too old for the hardest days, so the gentle ones are sold or given to families with children. Sometimes they are injured and have to be put down. And sometimes they experience complications that can't be explained.

That's what happened to Snips. I never saw another horse plunge his head into a water trough up to his eyeballs to take a drink. But he did. He filled his tanks by drinking deep, holding his breath as long as he needed in order to quench his thirst.

I suppose his unique drinking way was part of the reason I was so surprised. Bobby called and told me that Snips had died. He was dehydrated and the vet couldn't catch up with the need before the system shut down. I was surprised, and disappointed, and sad.

Snips was about as smart as any horse I'd ever encountered. We didn't just latch gates around him. No, we wired and tied and blockaded gates. Yet he was smart enough to outfox us on occasion. In our absence, he could find ways to get loose, or to get into a stack of hay behind double fences and gates, leave all kinds of evidence, and upon our return look at us as if to ask, "Who, me?"

He didn't have extensive training, but he was naturally sharp when working cattle, sensing their intentions like the best of cutting horses. But he was also aware of my intentions and directions as the one in the saddle. In short, he was fun to ride and work with. One day he was there, the next he was gone.

I guess it would be a perfect illustration of the old saying that the only sure thing in this life is death. Yes, we can add other things like taxes to the list, and personal items related to our experiences in life. But it's pretty certain: when you are born, you can take it to the bank, you'll one day die.

I wondered at the time, where's the glory in that? Where is God in the midst of the birthing and the dying, in the gift of a friendship that ends in the separation of death, in being brought together and then torn apart?

Yes, he was just a horse, like so many before him and so many since. I don't think I liked, or dare I say loved Snips more than any other I built a relationship of trust with. But at that moment I was sad, and questioned as we all do at times, what now?

My youth sponsor for the high school group I was in many years before was an angel in poor disguise. Her spirit was and is that of such sweet grace that you could see Christ living in and radiating through her. I believe it was in her that I first recognized the One and only thing I needed to cling to in this life.

It was in the witness of Claudia that I was taught to see what I saw in her in others, like my parents and grandparents and friends, and even in my younger sisters. In her I saw what it meant, and how it was possible that a person might be so consumed by building and sustaining a personal and intimate relationship with God in Christ that s/he couldn't help shining like light in the darkness!

It was in her I first saw evidence of that One, the only relationship that makes it unnecessary to understand, and liberating to simply trust God. In that trust, that true relationship of give and take, bless and blessing, joy and glory are made evident.

In that One relationship it was made possible for me to grieve the loss of Snips, to see the blazing glory of his trust in me and my trust of him, and to thank God for both! That relationship, with God in Christ, is the One thing worth counting on in these days we call life, and in the eternal hope that makes me believe in symphony composition all along the way home!

"Counting on One thing and One thing only!"
LUKE 10:38-42

Martha was so good, such a gracious host, covering all the details with excellence and kindness. But on that one occasion at least, she lost sight of the Guest in the details of the service stuff. For some reason the service stuff was more important than the presence of that Guest. She was giving away precious time in relationship to the details of duty.

How often we lose the opportunity of a given moment to know the enrichment of His company, excused by the erroneous judgment that He wants works instead of wonder to rule the moment!

REFLECTION

I suppose one of life's deepest regrets is found in those moments when, suddenly, we recognize that we've missed a blessing of God because we either weren't paying attention or were attentive to the wrong message. How often have I missed a chance to offer affirmation or praise to another because I was so wrapped up in comparing my own value to theirs?

The judgments of this world are usually readily evident and easily discerned. Why is it so difficult for us to note and receive and discern and rejoice in the affirmations of our Christ, of the One born Prince of Peace, King of Kings, and Light of the World?

Why is a dollar or a zillion dollars in hand so much more apparently attractive to us than the endless abundance of joy, grace, and peace offered just over there, just beyond our awareness and our time? Is a divine promise not enough to dissuade clinging to meaningless worldliness? Is the promise itself not enough to cling to for dear life's sake?

"A Miracle!"

Hebrews 4:14-16
"Jesus is our High Priest, before whom nothing is invisible."

I've seen some miraculous things in my days as a cowboy. But I don't remember anything more surprising and miraculous than Milagro. That was his name, which I was told means "miracle." That he was, in more ways than one.

First of all, his mother had been taken to a trainer. She was brought back to the ranch three months later, and the following summer High Loper went to the corrals and found that miracle suckling his mama. It was like the Ellzeys had been blessed with an immaculate gift!

That was only the beginning, however, as when I met him, Milagro was a 2-year old colt that had not yet been weaned, or even had hands laid on him. Silly as I was though, I thought I'd spent enough time with horses, and seen plenty of horse whisperer videos, and read enough books like *Horses for Dummies,* to think I could gentle this handsome stud.

Upon receiving permission from Lawrence to do so, I built a round pen out of portable panels, placed one side against a sturdy wooden fence, managed to separate Milagro from his mama, and started working him round and round, clockwise then counter clockwise.

It was work that had to be done with patience, which I had an abundance of at the time, and I was having fun learning firsthand how this horse "gentling" business works. But I think Milagro had a different mind-set altogether, wondering perhaps, "I'm trapped in this round pen, being chased by a silly little cowboy, so, what now?"

Well, miracle of miracles, he jumped out of my round pen, that's what! He jumped with incredible grace and cleared the wooden section of that fence with ease. Not to be outsmarted or less stubborn than him, I stretched a rope between the two posts on the fence he jumped, raising the bar at least a foot, captured him back, and worked him again. But he tired of my good company and again cleared the rope-topped fence as though it were daily exercise. At that point it was I who wondered what next!

I then moved him to the front saddle lot, a smaller space with seven foot fences, and went to work again. Now outfoxed and trapped, Milagro eventually did what horse trainers who use the round pen teach greenhorns like me, what a horse will do: he finally got tired, or dizzy, or both, and stopped running, turned toward me, and with a little give and take into and out of his comfort zone, he began trusting that I wasn't out to get him. He joined up with me, and a friendship was born. It took all afternoon, but from my perspective it was yet another miracle.

I suspect that if horses could think like we humans, Milagro might have wanted, in his heart of hearts, for his mama to come help him! I know that feeling. Many times I asked for my mama's help. Sometimes, though, we think our needs are not desperate enough that we require help, sort of like a pull-yourself-up-by-the-bootstraps cowboy. At other times we might know from experience that not everybody is interested in helping. And sometimes we know that the task at hand is one nobody can deal with but us.

However, it's also true that there is One to whom we can turn, no matter what the challenge we face may be, and find divine help, wisdom, support, and courage. Like Milagro, if we will quit running from the One who wants to love us like a friend, and turn to Him in trust, we will also discover that no problem is too big when we ask for the help of our Heavenly Father!

No, we don't always get what we think we need, or what we want, but we always get God's perfect and divine help. With that, we can't go wrong if we will join Him in His mercy and receive what He wants to share with us. There, together with Him, we discover anew the miracle that His generous grace is glorious!

"A Miracle!"
HEBREWS 4:14-16

The roadway has been made clear and straight, the mountains laid low and the valleys raised up, for US?!?! The way Home has been prepared, a Holy traveling companion has been provided, and we are invited to keep our eyes front, focused on the Messiah, as we travel boldly toward our eternal destination!

Except when we don't.

REFLECTION

Horse "whispering" is really sort of a myth. When engaged in the "gentling" process, I didn't whisper to Milagro. No, when I had something to say it was said with clarity. I didn't want him to misunderstand. What I didn't understand in the beginning was that what I needed most of all was to learn his language, not the other way around! When I did that, when I learned what those ears were saying, and the foot placement, and the raising of the head, and on and on and on, he suddenly understood me better!

It's almost like a miracle: the more I understand about what God is trying to say, in the Word, in my trusted friends, in the presence of the Holy Spirit, the less I think I need to tell Him about me.

I'm so very glad I learned early in life that jumping fences for safety's sake is a valuable skill, but that some fences are not to be jumped. When I submit to the design of God's fences, I am wrapped in arms of generous grace. That's miraculous in the return of forgiveness, compassion, and contentment.

Sometimes, after the fact, I wonder why I ever jumped some of the fences I did, and can see clearly what I missed by doing so. While I can't go back, He blesses me with new beginnings.

"Old Eagle Eye"

2 Corinthians 5:16-19
"Open your eyes and SEE how God makes all things new!"

It was my turn to plow again. The weather was scorching, but the ground needed to be worked in preparation for planting. It was my turn to climb on that, er, darned machine and sweat the hours of the day away. The sad part of it was that the field most likely to turn up an arrow point had been worked the day before by Jill, so I didn't have that prospecting to keep me awake!

Not without a good measure of moaning thrown in, I finished my breakfast and walked about a half mile to the field, grateful that the old cab-topped tractor, with a busted air conditioner, had been fueled and greased the night before so I could just get to work – the sooner begun the sooner finished. Little did I know the treat to come.

It happened in the hottest part of that afternoon. I was digesting lunch and fighting to stay awake when out of the clear blue sky a shadow crossed the cab of the tractor. I was not necessarily surprised at first, thinking it might be a cloud or airplane overhead. But then it crossed again, in the opposite direction.

Curious, I began straining at the windows for an overhead view and was thrilled to see it. I had seen one on the Wild Kingdom or some show like that, and I'd seen one in textbooks and National Geographic. But I'd never seen one in the flesh, or in the feather!

I was awe struck as I watched a gigantic bald eagle overhead. He was soaring as though without effort, apparently checking out the road ditches and fence lines for a mouse or rabbit.

At first I couldn't believe my eyes, but then grew still with gratitude at the sight. A bald eagle in the Texas panhandle! This was a rare treat indeed. I stopped the tractor and just watched as that graceful bird swooped and rose and rolled and floated in the air. Then it happened. With his incredible eyes he spotted something from high in the sky above, then dived headlong toward the ground. In one wind-screaming streak of feathers he dropped his talons and seized a rabbit, climbed back to tree-top levels, and flew off down the creek to the east.

I never saw the eagle again. It was a tough sell convincing the others of what I'd seen. But their lack of faith didn't diminish in me the joy of those beautiful long minutes that kept me awake the rest of the afternoon!

As it seems to be in the larger arena of life, beyond the fences that define who and what a cowboy is, I have found that for the most part every person I know or have known is wondrously gifted in one way or another. Those gifts vary as widely as our complexions and temperaments, but in the cowboy world I've known some very gifted and multi-talented cowboys, and some who are especially gifted in one or two areas of cowboy life.

While I did not have a mature enough consciousness to remember Lawrence's exhibition of gifts when I was a youngster roaming the ranch with Stephen, I did come to appreciate much of what he brought to the plate when I worked the LZ ranch full time.

It was obvious to me that he knew a lot about a lot of different things and was a successful rancher. But in reflecting on those years it now occurs to me that the one thing I never saw him miss was a count. I was even embarrassed a couple of times when after he and I counted a pasture of mama cows and calves my number was different from his, and his was exactly on the money. He simply had a true gift that I had not yet cultivated.

I'm grateful to believe that the Lord never misses a count either. I can't remember the first time I heard the phrase and I'll never forget the comfort it brought when I was told that not only does God count it all joy when we children choose faith and trust as a way of life, but that everyone counts to God – everyone.

God's choice was to bless us all with a gift of equal value when He chose to reconcile the world through Christ, counting every sin forgiven in the life, death, and resurrection of Jesus, not counting trespasses, debts or sin against believers. God's count provides that we might live in union with Him and with one another.

God too has an eagle's eye, and I count divine grace among the many gifts I've been blessed to receive, as well as one that will help fashion my praise report to the angels upon my return home. The bald eagle in the Texas panhandle will ever serve to remind me of the gift of such vision and promise.

"Old Eagle Eye"
2 CORINTHIANS 5:16-19

Because of God's love for us in Christ, we of faith become a new creation, leaving the past behind, and moving into a lifestyle and ministry of reconciliation.

It's that moving part that's such a challenge, getting up from the familiar and moving out in trust and faith of something that can't be bought and carried in the back pocket.

REFLECTION

In my younger faith life it used to bother me some that God never missed a thing. There was a time in fact when I thought I couldn't get away with anything, and was even scared of a God who kept score of my mistakes and sin.

The first time I shared a count with Lawrence, I was yet young enough that I was worried what he would think of me if I didn't get it right, so I counted with a measure of anxiety!

I thank God today that Lawrence never chastised or laughed at me when he got a count right and I missed it. I thank God today that God doesn't count my sin against me, but in Christ has made me a new, forgiven man whom He calls "son."

And I thank God that as my account with God has been reconciled in the life, death and resurrection of Jesus, God now gives me a part in the ministry of reconciliation in this world; that is, I am called to be forgiving as I've been forgiven, and leave the judgments of reconciliation to God.

Why is it that this world seems to invite us, moment by moment, to judge the worth of our lives and lifestyles by a standard of comparison with the uppity neighbor? Why do people in political and economic and sometimes spiritual leadership invite us to believe they know us better than God knows us?

What is a ministry of reconciliation any way?

How am I supposed to reconcile, or make right, anyone's account with me? Is it really as simple as forgiveness . . . though I might argue that forgiveness is not simple at all?

Is there anything more fulfilling in your life than a moment in time when you know you have said or done something that called a friend or neighbor or sibling back to the way of faith and forgiveness, and they have come with joy?

Old Eagle Eye

"Snake Dancin'!"

Matthew 7:15-20
"You will know the type of tree by the fruit it bears."

Other than those old Three Stooges spoofs, or the Bob Hope movies that used a snake charmer and a cobra rising out of a basket to the music of an oriental flute, I've never seen a snake dance.

But I've been party to dancing around a snake, and I've sure seen Tom dance a high-stepped prance!

It was late winter, or early spring, I don't remember which. But it was both still cold enough to bundle up a bit against the breeze, and warm enough to begin irrigating the small patch of alfalfa on the Dutcher place.

The field was about 8-10 acres as I remember, flat ground just up from the creek, and a good spot for a little more alfalfa than the 30-acres closer to the home place. This particular season about half of those acres had been planted to a hay grazer for winter pasture while the rest was in the alfalfa. So the ground was divided with electric fence.

Last summer's late weeds were now dry and brittle, but

219

also knee deep in some places, especially up near the irrigation pump stand. It was there that Tom and I were headed that morning, to clear out those weeds and lube the pump. Afterward we were going to lay out pipe for the first watering of the season.

As we were walking to the back side of the pump stand, with just enough room between the stand and the electric fence to maneuver without getting bit by that fence, I heard Tom muttering something about needing to keep our eyes open for rattlers that might be out trying to warm up in the early morning sunshine.

About that time everything smooth in the morning busted loose in the most amazing high-stepping I'd ever seen a cowboy offer! While I busted a gut with uncontrollable laughter watching, it wasn't funny at all.

Tom had looked down, to watch his step as he told me to do, and exactly in mid-step, half his weight pushed forward, and just beyond the point of having the power to step back, he spotted a 6-foot rattler crawling directly below his stride! With an urgent desire not to land on that snake, and a contorted effort to step back while at the same time also stepping forward, he fell off balance just enough that he swayed to his left and bumped the electric fence. The shock jolted his whole system enough that it forced him to react by twisting to the right, an action that blew him against the back of the irrigation pump stand and caused another shock to his now willy-nilly twisted body. All I could do was laugh until I cried, watching him try to regain some measure of control and not step on that darned snake!

I don't remember if he went to the chiropractor the next day, but I do remember that he should have! I suspect that his spine may have been as crooked as that silly snake's body was when it instinctively wound itself up in strike mode, wondering what the heck was going on up there above him!

Tom slowly recovered his composure. I apologized for laughing, and after I retrieved a shovel, that dangerous, venomous, stirred-up snake was quickly dispatched.

You know, some snakes are good. Sure, a defensive bull snake can hiss in a way that sounds remarkably like a rattler. But a bull snake's life, spent chasing mice, does farmers and ranchers a favor. Grass snakes eat grass hoppers. But rattlers – if they're good for anything other than scaring the begeebers out of innocent cowboys, mouse catching aside, I'm not sure what that good might be.

It's rather like with us humans sometimes. We need to keep our eyes peeled, so that we can avoid the dangerous among us. Are they helpful, friendly, courteous, and kind, like a good Boy Scout? Or are they filled with poison? What kind of fruit do they bear, or what kind of havoc do they wreck? Dances with any kind of rattler can be a bummer and are well worth avoiding, no matter the contortions and pains it might cause!

"Snake Dancin'!"
MATTHEW 7:15-20

It's simple: an orange tree produces oranges, an apple tree brings forth apples, an olive tree bears olives, and the tree of life . . . well, that's a choice we bear! And there's no way of escaping the truth: a tree is known by its fruit.

REFLECTION

My grandmother used to tell us kids, "You'll forever be

known by the company you keep." Early on I had no idea what she meant. It was just one of those old person sayings that made no sense.

Then I went to college, naïve and innocent as I was, and found myself in the company of young guys who seemed to have little or no interest in college work, just college pranks and pleasures. The instant I was invited to a frat dance and was enticed to go by the promise of, well, shall I say, promised a "date" for the night, I knew this was company I did not want to keep!

It can all seem so simple, and harmless, even when at times our actions are illegal and/or stupid, and/or unhealthy. Cheating on taxes, getting drunk every weekend, a single weed: what about the fruit of the tree here? Is snake dancing worth it?

When was the last time you produced a fruit of some sort that you were ashamed of later?

When was the last time you asked the Holy Spirit for guidance, and made perhaps a difficult but divine choice? What was the fruit of that faithfulness?

"Tools of the Trade"

James 3:1-5

"The tongue is a powerful tool for good - or not."

The old gate was on its last leg, or, its last hinge, and was in deep need of some TLC else it fall from the post into uselessness. Somebody needed to fix it!

So I surveyed the situation. It was one of those corral gates, a big one stretching out across an eight foot opening in the fence, and was about four feet tall. It had a tie back of twisted wire that helped hold its weight, stretched from the far top corner up the gate, up the old telephone pole post to about ten feet high. That tie back was in good shape.

But the gate itself had been swung open and shut, and busted up by wild and crazy heifers and agitated steers, and climbed over by cowboys and kids so many times that it was coming apart in those critical spots right around the hinges.

It didn't look to be such a tough job. It was just one of those little things that when ignored can become a bigger problem than it needed to be, and it was at that point. I decided I needed to replace two 2X6 hinge boards, and to use screws instead of nails this time.

The gate came down easily enough, the boards were replaced without much trouble, and in no time at all, only about four hours anyway, the gate was fixed. I pushed it open, then closed, found it working fine, and shoved it up snug to the latch post to close it. The latch. It was coming apart too! But that fix didn't take long, just time enough to replace the eye-hook, and then nail a new hook on.

That was easy enough too until, until the hook end decided not to cooperate, to jump loose from my now tired grip, aggravate me into deciding I could solve the problem by hitting it harder, loosing my cool just a tiny bit, and missing the target just far enough to totally smash my thumb!

Needless to say, that final small detail of the job was finished with deep pain and suffering, and anger and pain, and misery and suffering! How could I have been so careless with a powerful tool like that hammer in my hand?

As I sat in the house with my quickly blackening thumb in a glass of ice water, it dawned on me how important the tools of the trade are. Hammers and screwdrivers and nails and wood and wire for the fences, whips and syringes and branding irons for the cattle, saddles and blankets and shoes and brushes and bridles for the horses: all are critically important to the work of a cowboy. Each performs specific jobs, and the use, or abuse of each can create a smooth operation, or bad rodeo damages that are harder to fix than do right the first time.

Spurs, for example, were not invented so that a cowboy could exert power and control and authority over a horse. They were invented for use as reminders to horses in training or already well trained that the cowboy takes the lead.

Bridles, of all shapes and forms, serve the graduated purposes of training and restraining the inexperienced or the stubborn horse, and teaching or reminding the trained or untrained how to follow the lead of the rider.

And every such riding tool must be used with wisdom and patience to encourage and build trust between a cowboy and his mount, the trust that makes cowboyin' work.

Sad, how sometimes cowboys who need that same kind of encouragement and training from the Master of all masters, forget that horses are not beasts or slaves but partners in each day's journey. Likewise, we are not slaves to The Master, but children, beloved children, being trained and encouraged by grace and kindness and mercy, so that we also might be gracious, kind, and merciful.

That's where we children find the glory of our Father most evident. That's where we live that glory out in building trust between us, as between cowboy and mount. Grace and kindness and mercy are divine tools of His trade, and ours!

Tools of the Trade"
JAMES 3:1-5

The simple tongue . . . like a bit or a rudder, has power beyond its obvious size limitations! If you're going to open your mouth and assume any measure of authority in the words you speak, you better be darned well certain what your tongue speaks is the truth, for you will be held accountable.

O sure. Right! The tongue has that kind of power? Yup!

REFLECTION

I take most tools for granted, unless they cease to work for me. Or when I abuse or don't use them properly! I guess I'll never ever forget smashing my thumb that day. But I'll also never ever never forget that it was a hammer in the hands of an angry cowboy that did the damage!

It's like that with the tongue too. In the mouth of an angry cowboy, worse things than thumbs can get busted. Character is formed by God's tools of forgiveness, mercy, grace, healing, wisdom, and kindness. Even though cowboys are called of God to use those tools as we live among our brothers and sisters. When we slip, when we use the tongue in a hurtful way, it always seems to come back and bite us!

When was the last time you were injured by a tool? Was it a tool malfunction or a mental malfunction on your part? If it was on your part, did you learn an unforgettable lesson, or have you done the same again since then?

As painful as a busted thumb can be, even more painful can the cutting and destructive power of the tongue damage relationships and hopes. Never forget the power of your tongue in the lives of your circle of influence. Take seriously the call of God to use it with forgiveness, mercy, grace, healing, wisdom, and kindness and you will be held accountably blessed!

"Rodeo"

Matthew 5:43-45
"You are made children of God by love and love alone."

Ever so often, not frequently mind you, just ever so often, each of us tends to get the big head, to carry the notion that we're better than someone else, or that our mistakes or challenges aren't as severe as others.

Before I'd ever been invited back to contestants' row at a rodeo, I'd heard stories about how to tell the difference between rodeo cowboys, according to their special skills.

For example, I was once told that you could tell a calf roper or a barrel racer by the fact that they tended to drive the expensive rigs, the big Dodge or GMC units with slick in-line trailers behind.

Those who rode bareback or saddle broncs typically drove the Ford or Chevy trucks that were at least 5 to 7 years old, and their extra long trailers were nice but in need of a paint job.

As for bull riders and steer wrestlers – well, I was told they drove beat down trucks with identification logos long ago knocked off, fender wells so deeply bent that they had to be careful going over bumps or ditches so they wouldn't blow out tires, and trailers that were held together with bailing wire and a prayer.

Through the intervening years, though, I've discovered that such tales are not true now, even if they used to be. Seems to me that cowboys and cowgirls today tend to drive, old or new, well-equipped vehicles with accessible and efficient trailers and to dress with function instead of appearances in mind.

That makes sense to me, too, because in any given event it's possible, at the unexpected turn or jump or slip of the animal in question, the dirt to which they can come face to face is the same dirt for every performer. It's as true for a barrel racer whose horse slips as it is for a steer wrestler who glides off his horse, misses his calf, and ends up face down. Both of them, cowboy and cowgirl, end up in the fertilizer!

Part of being justified in claiming to be a cowboy may indeed be linked to whether or not a guy or gal can verify that he or she has been down there, down in the dump of mixed manure and dirt, which makes everyone who's been there look and smell quite the same: like a working cowhand.

Just as it is in life for all of us, whether related to the rodeo circuit, the rodeo out in the back lot, or the rodeo we face in this world no matter where we are: there are times when we just end up being dumped.

Where's the glory in that?

It happens to each of us, many times, sometimes more painful than others, but each time uninvited though perhaps not always totally unexpected. The glory, those things that will make for humor or delight or solemn gratitude in our Angel

Reports, is in the capacity to get up and give it another go.

We don't *do* glory anyway, not true, divine glory. We can only invite the Spirit of the Living God to make divine glory known in and through us. Sometimes the *bestest supremest* examples of that kind of glory are made manifest in and through us during and after one of life's rodeos, when the dumped get up from the fertilizer that makes us all equal and go at it again.

"Rodeo"
MATTHEW 5:43-45

Love means never having to say, er, to, well, love means that when you love everybody and are even praying for your enemies, then you're acting like the Messiah; then you will be children of the Living God. And why not? After all, God treats us every one just exactly the same, offering us each divine gifts of forgiveness and love. Now I don't know about you, but as hard as that may be at times, the payoff seems well worth the effort.

REFLECTION

There are great equalizers in this life. Death, taxes, rusty barbed wire fence, crazy heifers, and busted trailer springs: they each make of us the same fallible dirt-faced and weary laborers. There's just no escaping the truth that we're known by the company we keep, and cowboys and cowgirls look and smell all the same when they gather themselves up from being piled into the arena floor.

Maybe that's a part of what I love about the life. Yes, there are distinctive differences, particularly in skills. But the bottom line is that we love the work enough to keep at it, no matter how hard we may fall or how dirty we may get. For this reason, it's not hard to love those who share a love of the lifestyle.

But how about those sometime stuffed shirt fellers in the bank who hold our land liens, and our vehicle loans, and our stock in the sway of the markets? We're supposed to love them, too!

The payoff is worth it though, because loving others like Jesus loves us is evidence to the world that while we may appear to be married to the ranch, we're actually children of another world, and looking forward to green pastures forever!

Who persecutes you? How? What's your response?

Who do you persecute? How? What's God's response?

"Cut and RUN!"

1 Samuel 16:6-7
"We judge each other by sight; God judges us by what's seen in our hearts."

There was a moment, just a moment mind you, "because cowboys can't be afraid, or can't admit it when they are!" There was just that one moment, when I had to choose to stand my ground or to cut and RUN!

Really, there was no choice. Any logical, sensible, wise, honest, committed and sane cowboy like me would, without thinking, cut and run. After all, there I was, all 150 pounds of me dripping wet, with summer's sweat, facing an agitated 1900-pound solid black block of angus muscle with a wimpy worn cowboy whip, demanding that this brute, who wanted nothing to do with jogging down a runway toward a catch chute for a vaccination that would help insure his vibrant and bulging good health, go there anyway!

Suddenly, in the midst of my cogitating, he snorted again, and mustering all the wisdom and cowboy stealth in my wiry body, I bolted and jumped for the fence just in time for his quick rising nose to give me an assist across the heal of my left boot that launched me plumb over the top rail as if that's what I'd planned myself.

When I was out of harm's way, and Tom and Jill had stopped their laughing, we mapped out a new strategy. We decided to crowd that majestic beast into a tight corner pen with the 15 cows needing the same vaccine, so that he couldn't move if he'd wanted to. Then Tom would reach over the fence and sting him in the hind quarter as quick and simply as possible.

It worked! Immediately upon opening the gate to that pen, that black beast blasted through that small herd of bovine beauties and dashed for the outside fence, cleared its six feet of wire with ease, and was free of the lot, and of us.

That evening, as I massaged some horse liniment into my sore left leg, I was blessed with a new awareness. At that point, safe in the welcome confines of a comfortable ranch house, I could see that bull from a different perspective, from the perspective of, say, an artist.

He had muscles on his muscles. He was only three years old and bound to grow even perhaps a third layer on top of the other layers of power. He was more athletic than I could ever dream of being. In truth, the grace with which he cleared that fence on the way to his pasture freedom was incredible, a thing of wonder to watch. It was awesome.

His awesomeness was what brought me full circle. I'd started this day in awe of such a huge and strong animal. I'd then progressed around a circle of data gathering and choice making, passed a single solitary fleeting cowboy instant of fear, into a bull-assisted manned flight over an 8-foot rail fence, across the joy of the job completed, to wonder at his amazing leap to freedom, and back to awe at his sheer presence.

I remember him today as perhaps the most beautiful bull I've ever encountered. I expect that when I make my angel report upon my return home that his majestic stature will be expressed in words of thanksgiving, that the God who created all of life, all of what's known and as yet unknown to us, would give divine and intimate care to the making of an animal such as the only one who ever made me just up and choose to cut and run!

I still believe that was a wise choice in that moment. I also believe that experience taught me a valuable lesson in awe-application. It seems now that God is not capable of anything less than awesome! So from God I choose not to cut and run, but to stay close to and to trust in His awesome grace.

"Cut and Run!"
1 SAMUEL 16:6-7

It's obvious that this world relies heavily on what it sees: whether you drive a Caddy or an old Ford, what you're wearing and how you comb your hair, if you're obviously self sufficient or a transient/homeless/needy outcast, where you eat out and what neighborhood you live in. It goes on and on, doesn't it?

In the midst of all that we hear a word of divine counsel: the Lord looks only upon the heart, on the inside, at the character inside!

REFLECTION

Mercy, that bull is still as large in my mind today as it was that day so long ago. He looked like the king of the ranch, the power of the pride, the bull of the woods and plains and panhandle all rolled into one. He was simply awesome!

And yet, I hope that what the Lord sees in my heart is equally awesome: the love and gratitude I bear, the hope of divine hope fulfilled, the desire to please Him in all I think and say and do. After all, that's pretty much the only chance I've got, for 5-11 and 150 pounds with thinning hair and manure-crusted boots isn't much to look at!

It's so easy to judge by appearances. When did you last judge wrong what you thought appeared to be true in a friend or stranger? When were you last judged wrong because of your appearance?

It's much harder to consider the heart of a person than the appearance. But does it make a difference in your interpersonal relationships when you do that – first consider the heart?

Ain't God's way awesome?

"The Illusion of Permanence"

Ecclesiastes 3:1-8
"There is a time for everything - there is a time for everything."

I went back to the ranch recently. It had been some time since I'd last been down to what I consider to be holy ground, at least for me. Things had not changed much on the outside. No, the place was not being used as we used to use it. The Trail Boss had recently gone Home. The grass and cultivated ground were now leased out. Fences were in need of attention in places. But overall, it was still the blessed ranch.

As I drove toward the house on the lower section, my mind was flooded with fond memories, and some not so fond memories! For some reason the first thing I thought of was when I returned to the place after graduating from college. I had a degree that said I could teach. But my heart yearned to be back here, doing the work that just got under my skin as a kid.

I longed for being in the saddle, working cattle, sharing in the fellowship of friends and family. Thankfully, that longing was soon fulfilled when Tom hired me, and the first job we did was round up a pasture, with my being responsible for riding south about a mile and then to push everything back north to the windmill. When that day in a saddle on Popeye's back ended, I was certain I'd have a sore rear for the rest of my life, or worse, be a permanent pain in the butt! Some might argue that that's what came to pass.

When I turned off the creek road and headed down toward the house, I was blessed with the sight of a clump of wildflowers, bright blossoms of tiny yellow, and a part of Fall's final fling at life before the killing frosts of Winter set in. Reminded me of how many times I'd been in a pasture checking cattle, or fixing fence, when I'd come upon a wild beauty that if not for my being there would have shown forth God's creative brilliance for nobody else but God. Those reflections are gifts that will live forever even if the flowers themselves didn't.

As I approached the house, I caught a glimpse of a deer, a doe dashing for cover down by the creek. In an instant she had bounded over a downed tree and was gone. It was funny how I remembered the flood that had caused that tree to fall, and how long the flood waters seemed to stay on day after day. It was as if the recent rains had created a new and bigger creek. Then they subsided, fell back to the usual creek banks, and revealed for all to see, trees and trash and leaves and fencing and sand piles up against the trunks of surviving cottonwood giants that withstood the water's pressures.

I parked the car, looked down the creek to the old saddle shed and corrals, and instantly relived that day when we dogged a 700-pound bull so we could brand, vaccinate, and cut him. He had some healthy short horns on the crown of his head and I drew head duty, to ride him out there as protection against those horns being thrown back on the wrangler who held that young beast's fore leg in his firm grip. Only problem was that bull had more muscle in his neck than I had in my whole body, and I was sort of tossed to and fro like a nuisance.

At one point my right foot found itself on the ground right in the spot where his head came crashing back to earth, thereby leaving his distinctive mark of disgust on the top of my foot. While I alternated ice and heat on my foot that night, I wondered if I might not have a permanent bruise there, to remind me how silly I must have looked as I flopped around at that bull's, er, steer's whim!

As I entered the ranch house, its familiar scents of musty dust that came with being shut up and unused for a couple of weeks sent a history textbook worth of content through my mind. I noted then and there that in some ways it's very true: the more things change the more they stay the same. Or is it: the more things stay the same the more they change? I can't remember!

Truthfully though, don't we learn over time that except for the glorious grace of God, isn't all else in this journey home part of an illusion of permanence? In the midst of that illusion, my, don't we get blessed when we see the hand of God there?

"The Illusion of Permanence"
ECCLESIASTES 3:1ff

A time for everything. Everything? Sure seems like it. If God says so, it must be so! There is a time for everything, including gather a grace report to share with the angels when we get home. What a report it will be as we consider planting and harvest, weeping and laughing, finding and losing, war and peace.

In the midst of it all, there is time for remembering and claiming the love of God as our very own!

REFLECTION

Simply put, I/we often wish some things in this life would never change. For example, we used to make homemade donut holes in the winter, and we could eat enough to make us sick, and not gain a pound. O for the pleasure of that kind of indulgence to remain the same!

Then there were those cool spring mornings, and cool summer nights, and mystically wondrous fall days, and magical winter wonderlands. Thing is, though, part of the wonder is in the way they change, not stay the same.

I've changed too, in lifestyle and livelihood. My faith has also changed, grown through the years of experiences that continually reveal the presence of our Loving and Living Lord to me. But there is one thing that remains the same through it all: the memories. The ranch too has changed. But the wonderful, nourishing memories, they are unchanging treasure . . . like the treasure of God's abiding presence.

What do you wish were permanent in your life? How have you adapted to the changes through the years?

What part does the unchanging promise of God's grace play in your journey home?

51

"Saturday Sunset Serenade"

James 4:13-14
"You don't know, can't know, what tomorrow will be like."

It had been a tough day. As can happen, and seems to happen more often than the alternative of a smooth day, this particular Saturday had been one challenge, one rodeo, one twang away from being a miserable, rotten, good-for-nothing day. Rough as it was to ride Popeye, this day was that and a hundred times more!

Perhaps we could have guessed it might be this way when we got started. After all, the cook stove broke down so all we got for breakfast was toast, cold cereal, coffee, and orange juice. There were no mouth-melted multi-grain pancakes, no perfectly scrambled cheese-dripping eggs, and no fat-laden salt-riddled bacon slab! Just toast, cold cereal, coffee, and orange juice – and we were supposed to survive the morning on that and not worry about what we'd get for lunch and supper?

But that was just the beginning. What followed in quick succession was a gate opened and escaped through by Apple, so we had to catch up the horses with the pickup that decided the first cattle trail we busted across was too deep for the right front tire which blew out. This explosion causing an hour delay as we hustled back to the machine shed for the spare that had been left there when we loaded out hay yesterday.

Then, when we finally got saddled to ride out and bring in the middle pasture for sorting the smaller keepers from the bigger steers ready for shipping to the sale on Monday, High Loper's mount took a spill trying to make a sharp turn to cut back a steer who didn't want to cooperate, and after tasting dirt was skittish and hard to handle the rest of the morning.

Eventually we did get the pasture brought down, but then we discovered that the float in the water tank had, for no discernibly good reason, quit working. That repair job had to be added and moved to the top of the list so that steers could be kept up until Monday.

Lunch was much appreciated, and the roast beef sandwiches that didn't need a hot stove went down fine. However, the egg timer we used for our daily power nap at noon was off kilter and after being set for 20 minutes went off after only 6 minutes of its soothing tick-tick-tick!

The afternoon included fiasco after disaster with a stampede back to the middle pasture by the younger steers, my horse trying to buck on our innocent ride back to the barn afterward, a saddle shed whose door didn't want to open, that spare tire showing forth a slow leak, my slipping and falling waist deep into the water tank when we repaired the float, and on and on and on!

By that now infamous Saturday's sunset, we were all totally wiped out, grateful that nobody was seriously hurt, and wishing that Sunday were already here. What a waste the day had seemed.

Then I heard them. It was a pack of local coyotes living across the creek up under the caprock, about a mile north of the house. Almost every sunset they set up with their crooning. It was a Saturday sunset serenade. With it came a reflection on my part, and agreement from the High Loper, Trail Boss, and M.F: this day could have been worse; and we did get our work done; and we didn't have anything to apologize for! Maybe, just maybe, as tough as it had been, it was yet also another amazing gift from the King of Kings.

We relaxed in silence, listening to the serenade, remembering today, knowing tomorrow was not guaranteed, and being grateful for the grace of good friends and the sweet sounds of what well could have been angel voices.

"Saturday Sunset Serenade"
JAMES 4:13-14

When we're in the middle of it, life seems as if it will go on forever and ever, amen! But the truth is, the only guarantee we have is this single moment. We best make the most of it, not take it for granted, and thank God for the chance to live it, no matter what it brings in the way of challenge or blessing!

REFLECTION

Some days are just a daze of comical conditions and results. Nothing seems to go right, and even moments of contentment can be interrupted when something else goes wrong.

Then, perhaps not often enough, we are given a glimpse of something unexpected that draws us back to the divine. Sometimes we are reminded of God's amazing grace in surviving such a day of dizzy dilemmas. And sometimes we are serenaded by an improbable wild crowd, whose music is sweet as angel voices!

When was the last time your whole day seemed to fall apart?

Were you blessed with resolution and calm before hitting the hay for the night?

Do you do anything when you rise each morning to remind you that this is a day the Lord has made, and we are invited to be glad in it?

"30-30 Vision"

Proverbs 20:6
*"Lots of people claim to be, but where do you see the faithful
and loving?"*

Yes, I know: it's supposed to be 20-20 vision, at least for those with perfect eyesight.   But the sight I recall with confusion is that sight I had down the barrel of my grandfather's old 1894 model Winchester 30-30.

It was a sweet gun with a kick that reminded you of its power without throwing your shoulder out of joint.   I'd taken the stock off and refinished it, cleaned and cared for it with tenderness, undoubtedly because it had been Grandpa Dan's, and I was proud to carry it.   But for the life of me, it confounded me to know that I could hit anything I aimed at with that treasured rifle except for coyotes!

Maybe that's where I lacked in the 20-20 vision category.   I mean, I could hit those oil well signs on the cattle guard rails at 200 yards, I could hit skunks, porcupine, and rattlesnakes.   I could blow cans off fence posts at 100 yards, and I could knock hedge apples off bois de arc limbs with ease.

But coyotes were a different matter.

I have a suspicion these years later that it had something to do with the fact that I never took aim at a coyote closer than about 75 yards, and I don't recall that one of them was sitting still with a target stitched to their hide. But my 30-30 vision aimed at coyotes may have also been influenced both by the fact that they looked a lot like the last pet pooch I owned, as well as by their serenading skills.

Except for the rare occasions when we heard about folks losing chickens down the creek, or a scrap between a watch dog and coyote (We never had to worry about that with Marshmallow!), they weren't much real danger or trouble. Even though they were usually pretty skinny and had a long, slender snout, they could even be considered kind of cute!

So when it came to my view of coyotes, my 30-30 vision was never as clear as a 20-20 vision that might have taken them out.

Such truth speaks to my heart as well as to my head, for I find it quite easy to be content with a 30-30 vision in this journey, and sometimes quite an ordeal to do the work that's best or only accomplished with a clearer 20-20 vision.

It's easy for me to forget what I believe is God's truth along this journey home: that I am here with a purpose, on an adventure planned in Heaven, with a mission of symphony composition in hand.

Flat tires and fat snakes, busted fences and wild heifers, dogs that yip and spook cattle, knee deep snow, miracles, and a Windrider: all these are parts of a large picture that point back to the Creator, if I take the time to look. I guess what messes with my mind is that I have a view of the Truth, of God's mercy and grace, of the invitation to this sojourn and its clear trail back home, and still manage to get caught up in the distracting details of the moment.

Where is the wider view? Why is it such a challenge to maintain a vision of home? I suppose it could have lots to do with the fact that we can get so wrapped up in the journey that we forget the destination, or that we get so focused on the destination that we forget the value of the journey! Either way, we lose the delicate balance between the here and the there, the now and the then.

Only in the company of the Comforter, and only with the guidance of the very spirit of the Living God within, could I remember when I was down on my knees digging sticky mud out of the wheel wells of a sadly stuck 4-wheel drive that perhaps especially when we're covered by life's muddiest experiences, the grace of God abounds as we remember that this is not all there is to it.

Only with a divine whisper in my ear could I believe that while I was unraveling the barbed wire that came loose as I was trying to mend that darned west pasture fence again, and wrapped itself mercilessly around my ankles and threw me to the ground with laughter (I promise that's what the wire sounded like – singing with laughter as it whipped and coiled toward me!), that any of us can find joy in the truth that it didn't wrap around my neck and face.

Another way to view the truth is perhaps offered by the poet in me.

> A cowboy's got to be mighty careful out there
> tending to the chores and critters under their eyes
> to make for certain the job's getting done
> no matter the challenges or pains they share.

Sure, a blue norther can overheat a cool temper
or a purple souther can blow the day's plans away.
But that's no viable excuse for forgetting the truth
that the grace of the Creator offers certain shelter.

Got to keep the eyes focused though, looking always
past the trials in hand to Mercy's gentle embrace
that enables rawhide exteriors to soften to the sounds
of Heaven's sweet songs that help clear the haze.

There, amidst the adventure of this amazing journey we're equipped with vision and memory and hope, for anticipating with miraculous joy the reunion to come when Heaven's gates before us we see.

With a view of angel choirs anticipating our return home, awaiting the glory reports gleaned from the adventure here, we are fully prepared for living this life with loyalty and love for both God and one another.

May the vision of the day be 20-20 then, clear, and focused on none less that the Creator, the One who guides with gentleness as Windrider carries us upon the journey that leads us Home.

"30-30 Vision"

PROVERBS 20:6

There is a distinctive difference between making a claim and being able to back it up with reality. For this reason, trust is not a gift. Trust must be earned.

REFLECTION

Tom has disappointed me more than once. So has Jill. So have MF and the Trail Boss, and Bobby, and Snips and Deuce and Happy and Popeye. And mercy, how I've disappointed them, and myself, time and again. In the moment when I recognize I've been looking at life's circumstances with 30-30 vision instead of 20-20 focus on the Giver of Life, I can get really upset with myself. But then the Giver reminds me that those moments are critical to the grace report: where was God in the midst of it all?

Time after time after time I've come to see again that while we humans may indeed disappoint each other, it is also true that God never disappoints.

God never disappoints! What a concept. And how true: in every dark cloud or dirty rodeo or dangerous branding or nasty fence mending, there is the Living God offering presence, wisdom, and courage. God is worthy of my trust. God is just simply worthy of my trust!

When were you last a disappointment to someone you care about? How did s/he handle it? How did you handle it?

How did you handle it the last time someone disappointed you?

Has God ever disappointed you?

Practicing the art of 20-20 vision as we search for God's presence and truth is a dynamic help to us as we look for the grace in every setting of life that will fill out our angel report!

For additional copies of

TAKE ME HOME, WINDRIDER

by
JEFF KNIGHTON

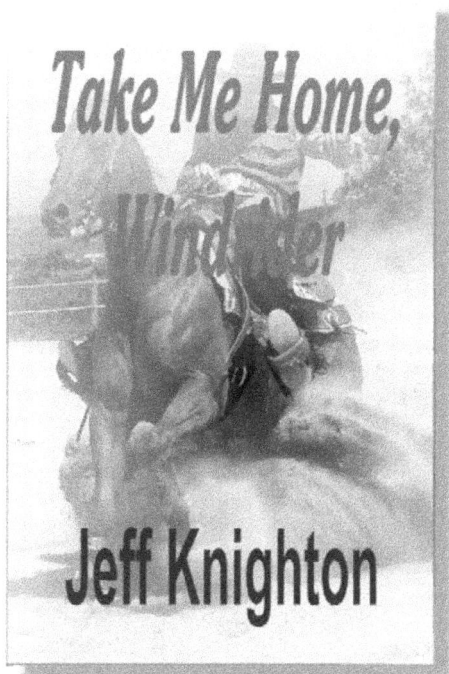

Please order from the following sources:
www.amazon.com
www.baalhamon.com
www.bn.com
www.thewindriderbook.com
www.joyandtruth.org
and at many other bookstores worldwide.

Also from Baal Hamon Publishers:

Worship That Pleases God - by James W. Bartley, Jr. (PhD)
February 2008, 360pp, 6' x 9'
ISBN 978-075-688-4 (Paperback: US $17.99, UK £13.99)
Category: Non-fiction

James W. Bartley *Jr.* has gone beyond the common *status quo* to explore a subject that most authors do not have sufficient experiential credentials to delve into. He practically reflects on his more than 60 years experience of walking with God to bring many into an awe-striking deeper communion with God. His book, *Worship that pleases God* gives an accurate insight into the inexhaustible subject of Worship – as an invaluable asset in the Man-God relationship. Being a retired Professor of theology, Dr. Bartley has successfully made a holistic and unassailable exposition of worship – as a theme that finds its root in the book of Genesis and continues to Revelation in the Bible, while his academic perception lends credence to his work. *Worship that pleases God* is not just a book that enriches the knowledge of inquisitive readers; Dr. Bartley has carefully sequenced it in such a manner that even the least motivated reader will simply find the wave of his discovered supernatural worship pattern so irresistible.

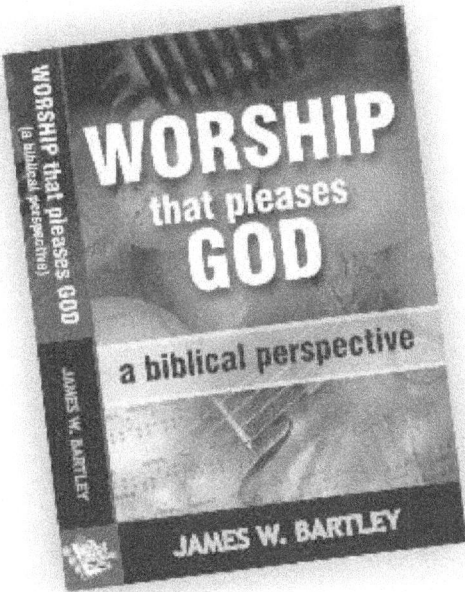

Order from www.baalhamon.com

The Fatherless - by Erin Inman
February 2008, 420pp, 5.5' x 8.5'
ISBN 978-075-691-4 (Paperback: US $17.99, UK £13.99)
Category: Fiction

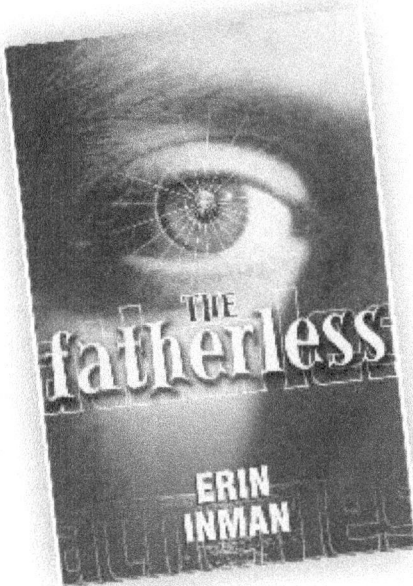

Nick Pierce, a talented young boy whose singular obsession is music, finds himself overturned from a lonely life with his grandmother in Wichita, Kansas to the rather strange atmosphere of life in Western Kansas with the father he had never met. Although a friendly neighbor couple takes *Nick* under their wing, circumstances in life and his father's attitude work against him.

In search for a way to fulfill his uttermost desires, he enters into a world of the unknown – a stranger world that leads him into questioning right from wrong. In the face of a life-threatening sickness, *Nick* wonders if life could offer him a little more, if music may still flow from his fingers, in praise to the Father-God.

Order from www.baalhamon.com

www.ingramcontent.com/pod-product-compliance
Lightning Source LLC
LaVergne TN
LVHW011219080426
835509LV00005B/221